TANKS

& ARMOURED VEHICLES

OF

WWII

TANKS

& ARMOURED VEHICLES
OF
WWII

Jan Surmondt

Published by TAJ Books 2004

27, Ferndown Gardens,
Cobham,
Surrey,
UK,
KT11 2BH

ISBN 1-84406-029-2

Printed in China.
1 2 3 4 5 08 07 06 05 04

CONTENTS

Char B1 heavy (Renault)

The Char B was the most powerfully armed and armoured tank available in quantity to any army in 1939. Work had begun in 1921 on a char de bataille to provide heavy support for the char d'accompagnement of the infantry and to deal with difficult enemy defences including tanks. The new tank was to be heavily armed and armoured and equipped with radio to achieve some tactical co-ordination in its semi-independent operations, though its role was still basically one of infantry support. Three prototypes were built from 1929 to 1931, these tanks carried a short 75mm gun in the hull front with two machine-guns, and two further machine-guns in a small turret. The hull gun could elevate and depress, but could not traverse from side to side, so the entire vehicle had to be turned in order to aim the hull gun. These prototypes were followed by 35 production Char B1s, which had heavier 40mm armour, more powerful 250hp engines and a new cast turret mounting a short 47mm gun.

France 1934
Crew 4
Weight 31 tons
Armament
One 47mm L34 Gun
One 75mm L 17 Gun
One 7.5mm MG
Speed: 17 mph
Upper Hull Front 60mm/20° Turret Front 56mm/0°
Lower Hull Front 60mm/45° Gun Mantlet 56mm/30°
Hull Side 60mm/0° Turret Side 46mm/22°
Lower Hull 60mm/0° Turret Rear 46mm/22°
Hull Roof 22mm/80° Turret Roof 30mm/72°
Hull Rear 55mm/15°

CHAR LEGER R35 LIGHT (RENAULT)

Designed to answer a requirement for a light infantry tank to replace the aging Renault F17 the specification of the R35 was firmly rooted in the age of trench warfare. The hull of the R-35 was built of three cast sections that were bolted together. The driver sat at the front, slightly offset to the left and had a large flap, also fitted with a vision slot, that opened upward. The one-man APX-R turret housed the commander/gunner/loader, who was provided with a fixed cupola with vision slits. A hatch in the rear face of the turret folded down to provide a seat as well as entry. Armament consisted of the short-barrelled 37mm SA18 gun (with 100 rounds) and a coaxial 7.5mm MG. The later production R40 used a slightly different turret with the more powerful 37mm SA38 gun, reducing ammunition load to 58 rounds. Armour protection was good, but the R35 was designed for the static warfare of WW I trench battles; it lacked a radio, had an inefficient one-man turret, its gun was ineffective against armour, and it was slow and short-ranged. In spite of this over 1500 were built and it was the most numerous tank in the French army in 1940.

Crew 2
Armament
Weight 10 tons
One 37mm L21 Gun
One 75mm MG
Speed 12 mph
Upper Hull Front 40mm/15° Turret Front 45mm/25°
Lower Hull Front 40mm/30° Gun Mantlet 45mm/30°
Hull Side 40mm/10° Turret Side 40mm/30°
Lower Hull 40mm/0° Turret Rear 40mm/30°
Hull Roof 14mm/75° Turret Roof 12mm/90°
Hull Rear 40mm/11°
Power plant
Renault four-cylinder petrol engine developing 82hp (61 kW)
Performance
maximum road speed 20km/h (12.4mph)
fording 0.80m (2ft 7in)
vertical obstacle 0.50m (1ft 7.7in)
trench 1.60m (5ft 3in)

CHAR LEGER H35 AND H39 LIGHT (HOTCHKISS)

Originally designed to meet an infantry requirement, this tank was actually accepted in to service with the cavalry. Despite production problems common to all French tanks in the period before World War II, about 1000 were built. It was similar to the Renault R35 but faster. The main visible difference was the use of six road wheels, rather than five. The driver sat at the right front with the commander (who was also gunner and loader) in the APX-R turret. Armament was a 37mm SA18 gun and coaxial 7.5mm MG. The H38 was an improved model with slightly thicker armour and a more powerful engine that caused the rear deck to extend almost horizontally. This increased the speed to 36 km/hr and, because additional fuel was provided, also increased the radius of action by about 10%. The final model, the H39 was fitted with a new turret, as in the R40, with the longer barrelled 37mm SA38 gun, which gave them some anti-armour capability. Like the R35 the H35 lacked a radio, overloaded the commander with duties, had an ineffectual gun, and lacked range but was capable of higher speed.

Crew 2
Weight 11 tons
Armament
One 37mm L21 Gun
One 7.5mm model 1931 machine gun with 400 rounds
Speed 23 mph
Range 150km (93miles)
Upper Hull Front 34mm/30° Turret Front 45mm/25°
Lower Hull Front 29mm/34° Gun Mantlet 25mm/30°
Hull Side 34mm/20° Turret Side 40mm/30°
Lower Hull 34mm/0° Turret Rear 40mm/30°
Hull Roof 22mm/88° Turret Roof 12mm/85°
Hull Rear 22mm/30°
The standard light tank used by the French cavalry in 1940. About 800 built. Some had the same turret as the R35.

CHAR S-35 MED. (SOMUA)

Among the specifications issued by the French Cavalry in 1931 was one for an automitrailleuse de combat to support the smaller AMD (armoured cars) and AMR (reconnaissance tanks) in its new mechanized formations. The original requirement turned out to be inadequate and the first two Renault AMC were built only in limited quantities. New specifications appeared in 1934 and these required a heavier 13,000-kg (12.8ton) vehicle with improved 40-mm armour mounting a 47mm or 25mm gun.

The tank that met this specification was already under development by SOMUA (Societe d'Outillage Mecanique et d'Usinage d' Artillerie) based on the existing CharD mediums. The first prototype of the AMC Somua Type AC2 was demonstrated in August 1935 and was accepted for service as the Char Somua Modele 1935S. The SOMUA S35, as it was generally known, was one of the first tanks to enter service with the newly mechanised French cavalry of the mid-1930s. It was a very advanced vehicle for its time and many of its features were to become standard for future tank designs, such as cast, rather than riveted armour.

Crew 3
Weight 19,500kg (42,900lb)
Dimensions
Length 5,38m (17ft 7.8in)
Width 2.12m (6ft 11.5in)
Height 2.62m (8ft 7in)
Range 230km (143 miles)
Armour
Upper Hull front 36mm/22° Turret Front 56mm/0°
Lower Hull Front 36mm/30° Gun Mantlet 56mm/30°
Hull Side 35mm/22° Turret Side 46mm/22°
Lower Hull 35mm/0°Turret Rear 46mm/22'°
Hull Roof 20mm/82° Turret Roof 30mm/72°
Hull Rear 35mm/30°
Armament
One 47mm L34 SA35 gun with 118 rounds
One coaxial 7.5mm Mle 1931 machine gun with 3,000 rounds
Power plant
S0MUA V-8 petrol engine developing 190hp (1417kW)

CHAR LEGER F.C.M. LIGHT

The FCM36 was yet another tank designed to meet the 1933 specification for a light infantry tank, in this case by Forges et Chantiers de la Mediterranee. It was more spacious than either the H35 or R35 and had a better radius of action thanks to the use of a diesel engine. The hull and the unique FCM turret both featured welded armour that provided better protection than the cast and bolted hulls and AMX-R turrets of the R35 and H35. The turret was larger and provided with a non-rotating cupola at the rear. It was designed to take a more powerful 37mm gun, but when that became available as the SA38 it was decided that the weapons would be fitted to new production tanks first, so the FCMs retained their less powerful L21 guns. The tank was also designed to accommodate a radio, but none were available. As a result, the FMC with its two-man crew, short gun and no radio, was only marginally better than the R35s and H35s with which it shared the battlefield. Only 100 were produced.

Crew 2
Weight 12.19 tonnes (12 tons)
Armament
One 37mm L21 Gun
One 75mm MG
Speed 15 mph
Upper Hull Front 40mm/50° Turret Front 40mm/20°
Lower Hull Front 40mm/45° Gun Mantlet 40mm/30°
Hull Side 30mm/20° Turret Side 30mm/20°
Lower Hull 20mm/0° Turret Rear 25mm/20'°
Hull Roof 13mm/85° Turret Roof 13mm/85°
Hull Rear 13mm/15°
Engine Berliet 90hp water-cooled diesel
Range 321km (200miles)

RENAULT A.M.C. 35 TYPE ACG1 LIGHT; RENAULT A.M.R. 35 TYPE 2T LIGHT

The AMC35 (automitrailleuses de combat), also known as the ACG1, was based on the earlier AMC34, which was in turn similar to the AMR35 but more heavily armoured. It was intended for use by the cavalry and was designed for a speed almost double that of the infantry tanks.

Only around 12 of the original AMC34s were produced before it was replaced by the improved version with new suspension and redesigned turret. Some were armed with a long 25mm gun in place of the 47mm, and were designated ACG2. The added weight of armour overstressed the drive train and the AMC35 was highly prone to breakdowns. The range was too limited for cavalry operations and the armour was considered too thin, although it was on a par with the PzKpfwIII. A replacement design, the SOMUA S35 was soon put in hand and as a result a total of only 47 were produced.

Crew 3
Weight 15tons
Armament
one short 47mm gun
one 7.5mm MG
Speed 25 mph
Upper Hull Front 25mm/45° Turret Front 25mm/20°
Lower Hull Front 25mm/45° Gun Mantlet 25mm/10°
Hull Side 12mm/0° Turret Side 20/mm15°
Lower Hull 8mm/0° Turret Rear 15mm/15°
Hull Roof 5mm/87° Turret Roof 5mm/85°
Hull Rear 5mm/10°

PANHARD AMD 178 ARMOURED CAR

This was widely considered one of the best armoured cars in the world when it was introduced at the start of WWII. The crew consisted of a driver at the front centre, the commander and gunner in the turret, and a second driver facing rear on the left. The transmission provided four speeds in both forward and reverse. The octagonal APX3 turret mounted a 25mm SA34 anti-tank gun and a coaxial 7.5mm machine gun. A small number were built as command vehicles, in which the main gun was sacrificed for a second, long-range, radio. The large wheels and four wheel drive gave the vehicle a high degree of cross-country mobility. In French and later, in German hands the AMD178 proved so successful that when Paris was liberated in 1944 production of an improved version, known as the AMD 178B was resumed. The 178B, with a 47mm gun in a new turret, remained in service with the French army until 1960.

Crew: 4
Weight: 8.5 tonnes (9 tons)
Road Speed: 72km/h (45 mph)
Upper Hull Front 20mm 21° Turret Front 26mm 24°
Lower Hull Front 20mm 0° Gun Mantlet 26mm 30°
Hull Side 15mm 0° Turret Side 15mm 26°
Lower Hull 15mm 0° Turret Rear 15mm 30°
Hull Roof 7mm 90° Turret Roof 7mm 82°
Hull Rear 15mm 3°
Armament
One 25mm L72 SA34 gun with 150 rounds
One 7.5mm machine gun
Length 4.79m
Width 2.00m
Height 2.31m

LAFFLY S15 TOE ARMOURED CAR

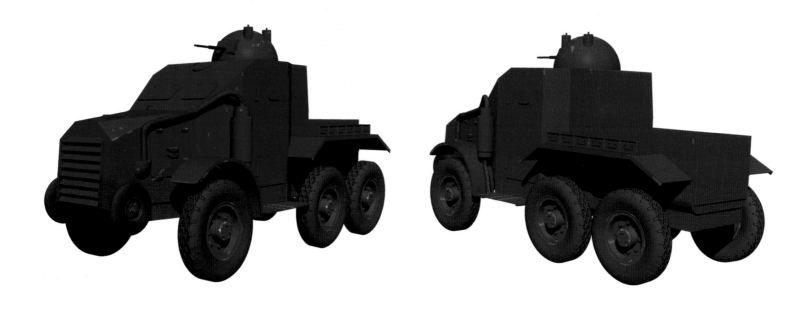

The prototype for the S15 TOE, the S14, was produced by Laffly at Fontainbleau in 1934. It was a six-wheeled armoured car based on their S15 chassis, which was originally developed as an artillery tractor and was then used for a whole range of vehicles. The S14 looked more like an APC than an armoured car since it had an open load bed at the rear and no turret, it also carried the small un-ditching wheels at the front end so characteristic of Laffly vehicles. The production version, the Laffly S15 TOE AMD was fitted with a distinctive small hemispherical turret on top of the body, not fitted on the prototype. Built in 1934, it weighed 5tons had a crew of three, mounted a single machine gun in the turret and was 15ft 2ins long, 6ft 2ins wide and 8ft 2ins high. It had a top speed of around 37mph and a range of 625 miles. It was also used as an armoured personnel carrier, in which role it carried eight troops. There were two main variants, a command version with additional radios and an SPG version adapted with a lower body and enclosed rear bed to mount a rear-facing 47mm AT gun. In all some forty five S15s were built of which at least twenty five were adapted for use in the heat and dust of North Africa.

Crew 3
Weight 5.08 tonnes (5tons)
Length 15ft 2ins
Width 6ft 2ins
Height 8ft 2ins
Maximum road speed 60km/h (37mph)
Range 1000km (621 miles)
Engine 2.3litre 4 cylinder Hotchkiss petrol

SCHNEIDER AMC P16 (M29) HALFTRACK
ARMOURED CAR

The P16 was a compact vehicle that was employed on reconnaissance duties. It used the Citroen-Kegresse half-track drive, and had un-powered front wheels. A large roller was fitted at the front to aid in crossing obstacles. In addition to the driver, the crew consisted of a commander/gunner and a loader. The M1928 trials models had a 37mm gun and MG mounted opposite each other in the turret. The octagonal turret of the M1929 mounted a 37mm SA18 gun and coaxial 7.5mm MG on one face, and had large flaps that could be opened for observation in all others. In 1940 a number of M1929s had the 37mm gun replaced by a 25mm Mle34 AT gun. The vehicle provided excellent observation, critical for a reconnaissance unit, but had no radio to transmit information back to where it was needed. Since it lacked the cross-country mobility of a full tracked vehicle and the speed and reliability of a wheeled vehicle, it represented something of a developmental dead end.

Crew 3
Weight 6.8 tonnes
Front Armour 11mm
Side Armour n/a
Length 4.83m
Width 1.73m
Height 2.60m
Armament
One 37mm SA18 gun OR one 25mm Mle34 AT gun
One 7.5mm machine-gun
Engine 60 horsepower
Road Speed 50km/h

PzKpfw I Ausf. A and B

The PzKpfw I, originally designed as stopgap, light, training tank formed a major part of the German Panzer forces until well after the beginning of World War II. The PzKpfw I dated back to a 1932 Krupp design for a light tank with four coil-sprung road wheels each side and a trailing idler touching the ground. A rear-mounted, 57-hp, Krupp M305 petrol engine drove through the front sprockets. This two-man vehicle, mounting two 7.9mm MG 13 machine-guns in a small turret on the right-hand side was chosen for production, with Daimler Benz superstructure, under the pseudonym Landwirtschaftschlepper (LaS) agricultural tractor to disguise its intended purpose.

Production began in 1934 by which time it had been fitted with smaller wheels and an external girder each side to carry the leaf-spring suspension of the rear three wheels and idler. Troop trials showed that the new tank was underpowered and an improved model was developed with a new larger 100bhp Maybach NL 38 TR engine. This improved the tank's power to weight ratio and ability to cover difficult ground but reduced the range to 87 miles (140 km). Weight and length were increased but armour was unchanged at 13 mm maximum, enough to protect against

small arms fire only. The new engine necessitated a lengthened suspension with five wheels and a raised idler. In 1935, with open rearmament, the need for subterfuge disappeared and the two tanks became Panzerkampfwagen I (MG) Ausfuhrung A and B; about 500 and 1,300 respectively were built. Despite their lack of firepower and protection, due to delays in the development of the PzKpfw III and IV production continued until 1941, and at the outbreak of war they constituted over a third of Germany's tank force. Many fought in Poland in 1939 and they also appeared in Norway and Denmark the next year. In the French campaign 523 were still on the strength of the Panzer divisions where good logistics made up for deficiencies in range. As late as the invasion of Russia and the campaign in the Western Desert PzKpfw I Ausf A and B were still in first-line service although by the end of 1941 most were relegated to their original training roles or had been converted to other uses.

The last version of the Panzer I to enter production was the 18ton, Ausf D (VK 1801) With 80mm armour and a heavy interleaved suspension the Ausf D was developed for infantry purposes in the summer of 1940. With its two machine-gun

armament and a speed of only 15mph (24 km/h), this design was not a great success and only 30 were built out of a total order for 130 tanks.

Crew 2
Weight in action 6tons
Maximum road speed 40 kph (24.9 mph)
Road range 140 km (87 miles)
Cross-country range 115 km (71.4 miles)
Length overall 4.42m (14ft 6in)
Width 2.06m (6ft 9in)
Height 1.72m (5ft 8 in)
Engine One 6-cylinder Maybach NL38TR (100 hp)
Track width 280 mm (11 in)
Wheel base 1.6m (5ft 5.75 in)
Armament
Two 7.92 mm MG with 1,525 rounds
Bow armour 13 mm (0.51 in)
Side armour 13mm (0.51 in)
Roof and floor armour 6 mm (0.24 in)
Turret armour 13 mm (0.51 in)

PzKpfw II

The PzKpfw II dated back to 1934 when a specification was issued for an improved light tank to fill the gap caused by the delay in development of heavier vehicles. A MAN design, the LaS 100 was chosen. The chassis had six small road wheels each side, sprung in pairs between the sides of the tank and an outside girder. A 130-hp Maybach engine drove the seven-ton vehicle via the front sprocket. The driver steered using the normal clutch and brake system as on the earlier LaS. A turret mounting a 20-mm KwK 30 automatic gun together with an MG 34 machine-gun was fitted and maximum armour thickness was 14.5 mm. From 1935 onwards several small pre-production batches were produced each incorporating successive improvements including a new suspension of five medium-sized, elliptically-sprung road wheels was adopted which became standard for the remainder of the series. With larger tanks still in short supply full-scale production began in 1937 by MAN, Famo, MIAG and later Wegmann. The first production model was the Ausf A this was soon followed by the B and C. During this production run extra 14.5-20-mm armour was added to the hull and turret front and a new angular nose appeared. A refit programme up-armoured

older PzKpfw IIs. In 1939 there were 1,226 PzKpfw IIs of all types in service, although by this time the deficiencies of the tank in armour and firepower had already become clear. Nevertheless, the PzKpfw II proved adequate in Poland and even in France as the major single type (950 tanks) in the Panzer Divisions that struck on 10 May. In spite of its shortcomings the PzKpfw II continued in production; although only 15 had been built in 1939 and 9 in 1940, 233 appeared in 1941. These were of a new version, Ausf F, with redesigned frontal plating up-armoured to 35 mm, and observation for the commander was improved by the addition of a turret cupola. Over 1,060 PzKpfw IIs were available for action during the opening weeks of the invasion of Russia but over such vast distances, and against a more heavily armed and armoured enemy, the weaknesses of the design were even more apparent. In order to make good the vehicle's deficiencies a few PzKpfw IIs received new armament, some being fitted with the captured French 37mm SA38. By April of the next year the number in action had slumped to 866 despite continued production, and increasingly they were relegated to reconnaissance duties.

The PzKpfw II Ausf D and E were special, 35mph, versions built in 1938-9 as Schnellkampfwagen (fast fighting vehicles) for the light divisions. These 250 vehicles had torsion-bar suspension and large wheels of the Christie type. However the new suspension had a disappointing cross-country performance and, in 1940, 90 were converted to Flammpanzer II flamethrower vehicles with two forward-mounted flame-guns and a small machine-gun turret.

Crew three
Armament one 20-mm KwK 30 gun with 180 rounds
one 792-mm MG 34 machine-gun with 2,550 rounds
Armour
hull nose 35mm, drivers plate 30mm, sides 20mm, decking 10mm, belly 5mm, tail 15mm;
turret front 30 mm, sides 20 mm, rear 15 mm, top 10 mm
Engine one Maybach HL 62 TR inline six-cylinder liquid-cooled petrol. 140hp
Speed 25 mph (40 km/h)
Range 118 miles (190 km)
Trench crossing 5 feet 7 inches (17 m)
Vertical step 1 foot 4.5 Inches (42 cm)
Fording 3 feet (90 cm)
Length 15 feet 9 inches (4.g1 m)
Width 7 feet 6 inches (2.28 m)
Height 6 feet 8 inches (2.02 m)

PzKpfw III

The specification for a 15ton tank, intended to be the mainstay of the new Panzer Divisions was first issued in 1935. A Daimler Benz design was selected, and ten production vehicles, designated 1/ZW Ausf A, followed; armed with a 37mm anti-tank gun, but with a turret ring of sufficient diameter to permit up gunning at a later stage.

There followed three years of development before the definitive arrangement of torsion bar suspension with six medium sized road wheels per side was arrived at on the Ausf E. A limited run of 41 Ausf E were built and after successful trials this design was standardised as the PanzerKampfwagen III.

By September 1939 98 Panzer IIIs of models A-E were available and a few saw service in the invasion of Poland. Initial production was slow in spite of a manufacturing programme that incorporated Daimler Benz, Alkett, Wegmann, Henschel, FAMO, MAN and MNH. By March of 1940 there were 349 Panzer IIIs of all types plus 39 command vehicles available for the invasion of France and the Ausf F had replaced the Ausf E on the production lines. The Ausf F was little changed from the Ausf E and was the first major production model.

Experience in France showed the PzIII to be seriously under-gunned, it's 37mm weapon being ineffectual against all but the most poorly protected of the opposing tanks. Krupp had begun development of a 50mm gun for the Panzer III in 1939, and forty Ausf Gs with the new 50mm KwK L/42 were rushed into action just before the end of the campaign in France but too late to have much effect. After France the fire power of the PzIII was further increased with the longer barrelled 50mm L60 anti-tank gun but new vehicles and Ausf Es and Fs in for refit continued to be fitted with the short 50mm L/42 to avoid production delays.

The end of 1940 saw the introduction of the next model the Ausf H. The Ausf H had the armour thickness of the hull front increased by 30mm with the addition of appliqué plates, and wider tracks were fitted, to offset the rise in ground pressure, caused by the increased in weight.

At the time of the start of Operation Barbarossa, the invasion of Russia, there were 1440 PzIIIs in service. Whilst the PzIII could cope with the older Russian tanks when it came up against the more powerfully armed and better protected T34 and KVI it became apparent that the up-gunning could no longer be delayed.

The new L/60 gun began to be fitted from November 1941 and the new PzIII, the Ausf J also featured improved armour of 50mm thickness all round.

The next model the Ausf L was unchanged from the Ausf J except for the addition of 20mm spaced armour plates to the gun mantlet and driver's plate. A tropical version, with special filters and ventilation, was produced and was widely used in North Africa.

The next model, the Ausf M, was the result of redesign to simplify the vehicle and speed production, the side vision ports being dispensed with, as were the escape hatches in the hull sides.

Crew 5
Engine Maybach HL 120TRM, 300bhp
Maximum speed 25mph
Armament
One 50mm KwK 39 L/60 gun
Two 7.92mm MG34 machine guns
Weight 20.8 tons.
Armour
Turret front 57mm, hull nose, driver's plate and tail 50mm, rear 30mm, sides 20mm Length 21ft 6ins
Width 9ft 9ins
Height 8ft 3ins.

PzKpfw IV

Originally the IV was seen as an artillery support vehicle, the PzKpfw IV was the only German battle tank to remain in production throughout the war years and it became the major such vehicle of the German army.. Development started in 1934 with Rheinmetall-Borsig, Krupp and MAN all being involved, the resultant design was produced by the Krupp as the I/BW Ausf A.

The specification had called for a tank of no more than 24 tons due to the limitations of the standard German bridge although the first vehicles only weighed just over 17 tons. The suspension, which remained standard for the whole series, was composed of four pairs of wheels and there were four return rollers; a standard 250-hp Maybach HL 108R petrol engine was fitted, producing a speed of 18.2 mph (30 km/h); and the crew consisted of five men, driver, hull gunner, commander, gunner and loader. The L/24 75mm gun was mounted in the turret with a co-axial MG 34 machine-gun; a second machine-gun was in the hull front, set back a little from the driver's position. The turret had electrical traverse. Hull armour was thin, 14.5mm on the hull and 20mm on the turret.

Production was slow to get under way, only 35 Ausf As were constructed in 1937-8, followed by 42 Ausf Bs and 140 Ausf Cs in 1938-9. These introduced HL 120 engines and increased armour thickness on hull and turret fronts. Both had new straight superstructure fronts from which the machine-gun had been deleted. The old layout was restored in the Ausf D, which appeared in September 1939, and 248 of this new model were ordered.

Combat experience showed the need for further up armouring and the next model, the Ausf E, production of which began in late 1940, had a thicker nose and appliqué plates added to the front and sides to bring protection up to 50-60 mm. On the Ausf E a new type cupola was adopted and was located further forward in the turret. 1941 saw the introduction of the Ausf F. This reverted to a single, and therefore stronger, 50mm front plate; a new ball machine-gun mount was fitted and the driver's visor was altered; weight was up to over 22 tons and wider tracks were fitted (400 mm instead of 380 mm) which necessitated a widened front sprocket

Altogether 278 PzKpfw IVs of various models were available for

the attack on France in 1940. They provided some useful support, being able to defeat the armour of most Allied tanks.

Limited production continued at Krupp in 1941 and by the time Germany attacked Russia about 580 PzKpfw IVs were available. Demand was stepped up with the proposed expansion to 36 Armoured Divisions in July but by April 1942 the number of PzKpfw IVs in service had barely risen above the numbers available the year before; more factories were brought into the programme and numbers finally increased from 480 in 1941 to 964 in 1942. But this was still hardly enough as it was becoming apparent

that the PzKpfw IV was the only German tank capable of up gunning to penetrate the well-shaped armour of the T34s and KVIs. A long 75mm gun, the KwK 40 L/43 tank gun was produced and fitted from March 1942 to the new Ausf F2 version of the PzKpfw IV; the earlier Ausf F now became F1. With a muzzle velocity with ordinary shot of 2,428 fps (740 m/s), and a penetration against 30° armour of 89mm, this gun allowed Panzer units to face up to the Soviet tanks on equal terms.

Weight 19.7 tons (20 tonnes)
Crew five
Armament
One 75-mm KwK L/24 gun with 80 rounds
Two 7.92-mm MG 34 machine-guns with 2,800 rounds
Armour basic:
Hull nose 30 mm, glacis 20 mm, driver's plate 30 mm, sides 20 mm, decking 11mm, belly 10-20 mm, tail 20 mm;
Turret front 30 mm, sides and rear 20 mm, top 10 mm
Engine one Maybach HL 120 TRM V-12 water-cooled petrol, 300-hp
Speed 26 mph (42 km/h)
Range 125 miles (200 km)
Trench crossing 7 feet 7 inches (23 m)
Vertical step 2 feet (60 cm)
Fording 2 feet 7.5 inches (80 cm)
Overall length 19 feet 4.5 inches (5.91 m)
Width 9 feet 7 inches (2.92 m)
Height 8 feet 6 inches (2.59 m)

PzKpfw V Panther Ausf G

In early October 1941 a specification for a new tank was drawn up, prompted by the appearance of the Russian T34, and intended to regain technological superiority.

Detailed specifications were issued in January 1942, the design was to include all the features of the T34 that made it such a formidable opponent: sloped armour, which increased the effective thickness of any given plate, large road wheels to improve the ride and a long powerful gun. In April designs were submitted by Daimler Benz and MAN; the MAN design being selected. The first two pilot models appeared in September 1942. Tests showed that the design was overweight and underpowered but the first 20 vehicles designated Ausf A were built to the prototype design in order to get production under way. To increase power a new HL 230 engine was fitted to subsequent production vehicles (Ausf D) together with a specially designed AK7-200 synchromesh gearbox and regenerative steering system to cope with the extra weight. Armour thickness was increased to 80 mm and the turret cupola was moved over to the right to simplify production.

Weight 44.8 tons (45.5 tonnes)
Crew five
Armament one 75-mm KwK 42 (Lj70) gun with 79 rounds and Two 7.92-mm MG 34 machine-guns with 4,500 rounds
Armour hull
Front 80 mm, sides 50 mm, tail 40 mm.
decking 15 mm, belly 20 + 13 mm; turret front 120-110 mm, sides and rear 45 mm, top 15 mm
Engine one Maybach HL 230 P 30 V-12, liquid-cooled petrol, 690-hp
Speed 34 mph (55 km/h)
Range 110 miles (177 km)
Trench crossing 6 feet 3 inches (1.9 m)
Vertical step 3 feet (90 cm)
Fording 4 feet 7 inches (1.4 m)
Overall length 29 feet 1 inch (8.86 m)
Width 10 feet 10 inches (3.30 m)
Height 9 feet 8 inches (2.95 m)

BERGEPANTHER A.R.V.

With the advent of the heavier Tiger and Panther tanks, existing German recovery vehicles such as the 18ton SdKfz 9/1 halftrack proved inadequate. Indeed to tow a Tiger tank it was necessary to use three SdKfz 9s in tandem. It was decided to develop a new recovery and the Panther was selected as the base vehicle. The Bergepanther first appeared in 1943. The Panther's turret was removed and replaced by an open superstructure containing a winch. A large anchor at the back dug into the ground to give the vehicle extra stability when winching. There was also an open machine. gun mounting on the front of the vehicle for self-defence. Bergepanthers entered full service in the spring of 1944, concentrated in the heavy tank battalions, and by the end of the war almost 300 had been produced. It proved to be the best German recovery vehicle of World War II.

Crew 5
Weight 42.000kg (92,400lb)
Length 8.153m (26ft 9in)
Width 3.276m (10ft 9in)
Height L74m (9ft)
Range 169 km (105 miles)
Armour 8.40mm (0.3-1.57in)
Armament one 20mm cannon and one 7.92mm machine gun
Power plant one Maybach HL210 P30 petrol engine developing 642hp (47B7kW)
Maximum road speed 32km/h (20mph)
Fording 1.70m (5ft 7in)
Vertical obstacle 0.91 m (3ft 0in)
Trench 1.91 m (6ft 3in)

PzKpfw VI Tiger

The Tiger's origins go back to 1938 when development work began on a programme to provide a successor to the Panzer IV. One of the prototypes produced by Henschel & Sohn GmbH of Kassel was the VK36.01 a 36ton medium tank, a design that would eventually form the basis of the Tiger. Initially there was little official support for the programme, however experience of British and French heavy tanks soon highlighted the need for a heavier tank. With the invasion of Russia on 22nd June 1941 clashes with the Soviet KVI and T34 made a new tank a vital necessity.

In the autumn of 1940 a contract had been awarded Porsche to develop a 45ton tank. In February 1941 Krupp were contracted to produce the main gun and turret. The first prototype of the new tank designated VK 45.01(P) was completed in April 1942 and the second in June of that year and was sent to Kummersdorf for testing. The hull was of all new design and incorporated an innovative petrol-electric transmission and the main armament was the 8.8cm KwK L/56. In the mean time Henschel had, on 28 May 1942, received an order to produce a modified version of their VK36.01 capable of mounting the 8.8cm KwK L/56.

This was to be done in such a short time scale that the only practical option was to modify the VK36.01 to carry the entire turret and gun assembly designed for the VK45.01. This forced Henschel to upgrade the design from the 36ton class to 45tons and eventually 56tons, a goal that was achieved with surprisingly little change in the original design. The first prototype, designated VK45.01(H) was completed in April 1942. Comparative trials showed Henschel's VK45.01 to be the better vehicle and it was subsequently selected for production. After an initial order for three pre-production vehicles the first production Tiger was completed on 17May 1942.

In operation the Tiger was, once the initial teething troubles had been corrected, a robust and reasonably reliable vehicle. It's cross-country mobility and ability to negotiate obstacles was equal to or better than most Allied and German vehicles of the period. Tactically it was to some extent limited by its voracious fuel consumption and most bridges would not support its weight. However, at the time of it's introduction the Tiger reigned supreme in battle.

Weight 54.1 tons (55 tonnes)
Crew five
Armament
One 88mm KwK 36 (L/56) gun with 92 rounds
Two 7.92mm MG34 machineguns with 5,700 rounds
Armour
Hull nose 100mm, glacis 60mm, driver's plate 100mm, sides 60-80mm, decking and belly 26mm, tail 82mm; turret mantlet 110mm, front 100mm, sides and rear 80mm, top 26mm
Engine one Maybach HL230 P45 water-cooled petrol, 694hp
Speed 23mph (37km/h)
Range 62 miles (100km)
Trench crossing 7ft 6ins (2.29m)
Vertical step 2ft 7ins (79cm)
Fording 4ft (1.22m) or with special equipment 13ft (3.96m)
Overall length 27ft 9ins (8.46m)
Width combat tracks 12ft 3ins (3.73m), narrow tracks 10ft 4ins (3.15m)
Height 9ft 6ins (2.9m)

PzKpfw VI Ausf. B King Tiger

In August 1942 specifications were issued for a replacement for the Tiger tank incorporating the latest sloped armour of the T34 and Panther, increased protection and a longer 71 calibre 88mm gun. It was hoped that this would keep German tanks ahead of any future Soviet designs in the gun/armour race. Both Porsche and Henschel were both asked to tender and the former produced modified VK 4502 (P) versions of his earlier Tiger (P). Interest was shown in a version with electric drive and rear mounted 88mm gun, but the need for copper, a scarce commodity in blockaded Germany, for the electric transmission resulted in the Henschel V K 4503 (H) design being chosen for service. Suspension was on the classic German principle with conventional torsion bars but used overlapped road wheels rather than the interleaved system of the Tiger I to ease access to the inner wheels and reduce the tendency to jam with packed and frozen mud. Resilient steel road wheels were employed for increased durability and to conserve rubber. As with the older Tiger two sets of tracks were provided, a wider set that reduced ground pressure for use in action and a narrow transport pair to bring the vehicle within the railway loading gauge.

Ordered in January 1943 the first PzKpfw VI Tiger II or Ausf B (SdKfz 182) production was under way by February 1944 when the first eight vehicles were produced by Henschel. The planned production target was 145 Tiger IIs per month but this was never achieved and the total production run was only 480. The first 50 vehicles carried the Porsche designed turret, the remainder the production Henschel turret with its heavier, better-shaped armour.

The Tiger Ausf B, known as the Konigstiger or King Tiger, was a formidable and huge vehicle. It was the heaviest, most thickly armoured and most powerfully armed battle tank to see service in any numbers during the war. But a price had to be paid; weight was increased by ten tons over that of the Tiger I and the highly stressed engine and transmission inevitably led to problems with reliability.

The Tiger II had made its combat debut on the Eastern Front in May 1944 and was in service in France by August of the same year. It was allocated in the same way as the Tiger I being either kept in independent battalions or being formed into the tank regiments of privileged Panzer divisions. With such a small

production run the Tiger II was never a common tank and, although the previously mentioned Ardennes offensive is usually associated with it, there were comparatively few in action.

Weight 68.7 tons (69.4 tonnes)

Crew five

Armament

One 88mm KwK 43 (L/71) gun with 80 rounds

Two 7.92-mm MG34 machine-guns with 5,850 rounds

Armour

hull nose 100 mm, glacis 150 mm, sides and tail 80 mm, decking 40 mm;

turret front 185 mm, sides and rear 80 mm, top 44 mm

Engine one Maybach HL 230 P 30 V-12 liquid-cooled petrol, 600-hp

Speed 23.6 mph (38 km/h)

Range 68.4 miles (110 km)

Trench crossing 8 feet 2 inches (2.5 m)

Vertical step 2 feet 9.5 inches (85 cm)

Fording 5 feet 3 inches (1.6 m)

Overall length 33 feet 8 inches (10.26 m)

Width wide tracks: 12 feet 3.5 inches (4. 72 m),

narrow tracks. 10 feet 8 inches (3.27 m)

Height 10 feet I1.5 inches (3.08 m)

PANZERSPAHWAGEN II LYNX

The prototype of the PzKpfw II Ausf L (SdKfz 123) Luchs (Lynx), the VK1303 first appeared in 1942, but it was the product of a long and complicated development story that goes back to 1938 involving both Daimler-Benz and MAN. The final design was a combination of ideas from several prototypes produced by both companies, in particular the VK901 and the VK1601. The prototype VK1301 in mild steel ran in April 1942, looking very like VK901. Various alterations were made to this first prototype and VK1303, the third prototype, was accepted for production at a weight of 11.8 tons, a reduction of a little over a ton on the first prototype VK1301.

Intended primarily for reconnaissance the Lynx was also given the designation Panzerspahwagen II (20mm KwK38) Luchs with the ordnance number SdKfz 123. It weighed 11.8tons, had a crew of four men, and was fitted with a Maybach III 66P six-cylinder engine, which developed 180hp. The drive was taken to the front sprocket through a six-speed syncromesh gearbox and controlled differential steering on the cross shafts. The maximum speed was 38mph.

Crew 4
Weight 11.8tons
Power plant Maybach HL66P six-cylinder engine, developing 180hp.
Maximum road speed 38mph
Armament
One 20mm KwK38 cannon OR one 50mm KwK39 L/60 gun
Armour 30mm front, 20mm sides

PzKpfw 35(t)

The Skoda LT35 was conventional in layout with a driver and a radio operator/machine gunner in the front, and commander/gunner in the turret. The turret mounted a 3.7cm Skoda A3 gun (for which 78 rounds were carried) and a coaxial 7.9mm vz37 machine gun. The turret was manually rotated, with a free-rotation disconnect lever for rapid traverse. The tank featured pneumatically assisted steering and shifting that made the driver's job easier, but added to the maintenance burden. The tank had a telegraphic radio and no intercom, but when the Germans took them over they replaced the radio with a voice set and added an intercom. The Germans also found room to add a fourth crewmember to the turret, who acted as a loader. One weakness of the design was the large-scale use of rivets in the construction: when hit by hostile fire these tended to fly off inside the tank with potentially disastrous results for the crew. Never the less the LT-35 was a good, if complex, tank for its time, with a powerful gun and adequate armour. It was used in the invasions of Poland and France, and 190 were available for the assault on Russia.

Crew 3 later 4
Weight 10.5 tonnes
Front Armour 25mm
Side Armour 15mm
Length 4.90m
Width 2.06m
Height 2.37m
Armament
One 3.7cm Skoda A3 gun with 78 rounds
One 7.92mm vz37 machine gun
Engine 120 horsepower six cylinder petrol
Road Speed 34km/h

PzKpfw 38(t)

The most numerous of the Czech tanks to see service with the German forces was the CKD/Praga TNHP LT38 in who's service it was known as the PzKpfw38(t). The four-man crew consisted of a driver and a radio operator in the front, with a ball-mounted MG between them, and the commander and gunner in the turret. The armament of the LT38 consisted of the 3.7cm Skoda A7 gun (with 90 rounds) with a second machine-gun in a ball-mount parallel to the main gun. The Germans replaced the original telegraphic radio with a voice unit and added an intercom. By the standards of 1939/40 it was a remarkably well-balanced tank design. However, the tank's automotive excellence was somewhat offset by its lack of growth potential due to the narrow hull. It could not be up-gunned, nor could a third turret crewman be added. However the chassis was kept in production until the end of the war and served as the basis of numerous self propelled guns.

Crew four
Armament
One 37.2-mm Skoda A7 (L/47.8) gun with 90 rounds
Two 7.92-mm MG 37(1) (Model 37) machine-guns with 2,550 rounds
Armour
Hull nose, glacis and driver's plate 25mm
Sides 15-19 mm
Decking 10 mm
Belly 8 mm
Tail 12 mm
Turret front and sides 25mm
Top10 mm
Rear 15 mm
Engine
one Praga EPA Model I in line six-cylinder, liquid-cooled petrol, 125hp
Speed 35 mph (56km/h)
Range 125 miles (200km)
Trench crossing 6 feet 1 inch (1.85m)

PanzerJager 38(t) (SdKfz 138/139) (Marder)

This was the first of several self-propelled guns to be based on the chassis of the PzKpfw 38(t). The conversion involved the removal of the turret, in its place a low superstructure was constructed to house a large anti-≠tank gun fitted with a three-sided shield. In the SdKfz139 the gun was the 7.62cm Pak36(r)(Russian 76.2mm anti-tank guns captured in their hundreds), and in the SdKfz138 it was the 7.5cm Pak40/3. Various improvements were introduced in the course of production, 194 of the SdKfz139s were built on the Model G chassis, the rest of the 139s and 275 of the SdKfz138s were built on the Model H chassis with a more powerful engine.

The SdKfz138 Ausf M was more refined, and was the first to be built on a new derivative of the PzKpfw38 chassis specifically intended for self-propelled guns. The engine was relocated to the centre of the hull, leaving a gun deck at the rear. This lowered the silhouette, reduced the overhang of the gun barrel and created more space for the gun crew. The hull machine gun, found in earlier models, was deleted in the 138M. Main gun traverse was 21° each side in the 138M and 139, and 30° in the 138H. Ammunition stowage ranged from 27 to 38 rounds.

Weight 10.5 tons (10.7 tonnes)
Crew four
Armament
one 76.2-mm PaK 36(r) (L/54.8) gun with 30 rounds
one 7.92-mm MG 37(t) machine-gun with 1,500 rounds
Armour hull nose and driver's plate 25 + 25 mm,
sides and rear 15 mm. superstructure front and
sides 16 mm, gun shield II mm
Engine one Praga EPA Model 111.125 hp
Speed 26 mph (42 km/h)
Range 115 miles (185 km)
Overall length 21 feet 1 inch (6.43 m)
Height 8 feet 2 inches (25 m)

JAGDPANZER IV

In June 1944 Hitler ordered that production of the PzKpfw IV should be abandoned to concentrate on its tank destroyer derivative, the Jagdpanzer IV, which had the 3,068 fps (935 m/s) L/70 gun of the Panther in a limited-traverse mounting. Early models of the Jagdpanzer IV were fitted with the L/48 75mm gun used in the StuG III as it took time to adapt the L/70 weapon for use in the new vehicle. Frontal protection was 60mm with 30mm armour fitted at the sides. Initially the Jagdpanzer IV carried a muzzle brake on the gun but as it was mounted so low, only four feet seven inches (1.40m) above the ground it produced a great deal of dust from the deflected blast and later vehicles had this deleted.

As soon as the new L/70 75mm guns became available they were fitted and armour thickness was also increased, the new model being known as the Jagdpanzer IV/70. Small numbers were in action by August 1944. Its powerful armament and extremely low silhouette made it a formidable defensive weapon, however, despite ambitious production schedules only 1,531 Jagdpanzer IVs of all types were constructed. They usually served with the tank destroyer battalions of Panzer divisions.

Weight 25.3tons (25.8 tonnes)
Crew four or five
Armament one 75mm StuK 42 (L/70) with 60 rounds .
Armour hull nose and driver's plate 85 mm, glacis 20 mm, sides 30 mm, decking and belly 10 mm, tail 20 mm, superstructure front 80 mm, mantlet 120 mm, sides 40 mm, roof 20 mm, rear 30mm
Engine one Maybach HL 120 TRM V-12 water-cooled petrol, 300hp
Speed 24 mph (38 km/h)
Range 200 miles
Trench crossing 7 feet 3 inches (2.2 m)
Vertical step 2 feet (60 cm)
Fording 3 feet 3 inches (1.00 m)
Overall length 27 feet 8 inches (8.44 m)
Width 9 feet 7 inches (2.93 m)
Height 6 feet 1 inch (1.85 m)

Jagdpanzer V Jagdpanther

The Panther had a small number of special versions; the most famous was the Jagdpanther (Hunting Panther) tank destroyer. This was developed in 1943 as a well-protected mobile mount for the formidable PaK43 88mm gun with its 3,708 fps (1,130 m/s) muzzle velocity and which could penetrate 226 mm of 30° armour at 500 yards (457m). The Nashorn was too lightly protected and Elefant too expensive, complex and for the task, so it was decided to use the Panther chassis with a low sloped front superstructure. The gun was fitted in the frontal plate with 11° traverse to each side, 8° elevation and 14° depression and a machine-gun was fitted in the right hull front for close in defence. A crew of six was needed: commander, gunner, wireless operator / machine-gunner, driver and two loaders for the heavy, clumsy ammunition. First called Panzerjager Panther (SdKfz 173) it received the designation Jagdpanther in 1944.

Production began in December 1943 and MIAG had it well under way by May using Ausf G chassis with an improved AK7-400 gearbox to take the extra weight. The vehicles were issued to special tank destroyer battalions composed of 30 Jagdpanthers, which were kept under central army control.

Weight 44.8 tons (45.5 tonnes)
Crew six
Armament one 88-mm PaK 43/3 (L/71) with 60 rounds and one 7.92-mm MG 34 machine-gun with 600 rounds
Armour front 80 mm, mantlet 120 mm, sides 40-50 mm, decking 17 mm, belly 20+ 13 mm, Tail 40 mm
Speed 28.5 mph (46 km/h)
Range 100 miles (160 km)
Overall length 33 feet 3 inches (10.13m)
Height 8 feet 11 inches (2.72 m)
Other details as PzKpfw V Panther Ausf G tank

JAGDPANZER 38(T) HETZER

The Hetzer was based on the well-tried automotive components of the PzKpfw 38(t) family, but had a wider hull, needed in order to allow traverse of the main gun. Even so, traverse was limited to 5° left and 10° right of centre. The main gun was the 7.5cm Pak39 L/48, for which 41 rounds were carried. A remote-control machine gun was mounted on the roof, with a 50-round magazine, and was aimed and fired by the loader via a periscope. The driver sat at the left front, the gunner behind him (aiming via a periscope), the loader behind him, and the commander on the right behind the gun. The Hetzer was a remarkable design, combining small size, well thought-out armour protection and a lethal gun. It was also very cramped inside, had poor visibility of the outside, and the limited traverse of the main gun, especially to the left, could create tactical problems.

There were three variants of the Hetzer; the Flammpanzer 38(t) in which the main gun was replaced with a flamethrower; the Bergepanzer 38(t) designed as a recovery vehicle for the Hetzer; and lastly the Hetzer Befehlswagen a command version of the basic vehicle with reduced ammunition stowage and additional radio equipment.

Weight 15, 7 tons (16 tonnes)
Crew four
Armament
One 75mm PaK 39 (L/48) gun with 41 rounds
One 7.92-mm MG 34 machine-gun with 600 rounds
Armour front 60 mm, sides 20 mm, decking and tail 8 mm
Engine one Praga EPA/AC Model IV, in line six cylinder 150 hp
Speed 26 mph (42 km/h)
Range 112 miles (180 km)
Trench crossing 4 feet 3 inches (13 m)
Vertical step 25 inches (64 cm)
Fording 3 feet (90 cm)
Overall length 20 feet 7 inches (6.27 m)
Width 8 feet 8 inches (2.63 m)
Height 6 feet II inches (2.1 m)

Jagdpanzer Tiger (P) Elefant

The Elefant was based on the chassis of the unsuccessful Porsche design for the Tiger tank. One hundred chassis had been constructed in anticipation of an order that never materialised; the contract going to the competing Henschel design. In order to utilize these chassis it was decided to convert ninety of them into tank destroyers. They were fitted with a heavily-armoured superstructure, mounting an 8.8cm Pak43/2 (L/71) gun. The gun had a traverse of 14° each side and could elevate from -8° to +14°. Initially the Elefant was not fitted with any secondary armament, it also had large blind spots to the sides and rear that permitted Soviet infantry tank killer teams to close with the vehicle during the battle of Kursk. To remedy these defects when the surviving 48 vehicles were pulled out of service in late 1943 for overhaul they were given a ball mount MG in the driver's plate, along with a commander's cupola. Extremely well armed and provided with thick armour, the vehicle was a formidable tank destroyer in a defensive role where its mediocre mobility was not such a liability.

Weight 66.9 tons (68 tonnes)
Crew six
Armament
One 88mm StuK 43/2 (L/71) gun with 50 rounds
Armour
Hull nose and driver's plate 100+100 mm, sides 80 mm, decking 30 mm, belly 20 + 30 mm. tail 80 mm
Superstructure front 200 mm, sides and rear 80 mm, top 30 mm
Engines two Maybach HL 120 TRM V-12 liquid cooled petrol, 530-hp
Speed 12.5 mph (20 km/h)
Range 95 miles (153 km)
Trench crossing 10 feet 6 inches (3.20 m)
Vertical step 31 inches (78 cm)
Fording 4 feet (1.22 m)
Overall length 26 feet 8 inches (8.13 m)
Width 11feet 1inch (3.38 m)
Height 9 feet 10 inches (3.00 m)

JAGDPANZER VI JAGDTIGER

The Jagdtiger (SdKfz 186) was the most powerful armoured vehicle to see general service during the war. It was German policy to build a limited-traverse mounting of a heavier gun on any given tank chassis and the King Tiger was no exception. A lengthened hull was used with a large fixed central superstructure armoured to a maximum thickness of 250 mm and mounting a 55-calibre 128mm PaK 80, a weapon that could out-range any other tank gun and penetrate any other AFV. Earlier models mounted the shorter 128mm PaK 44 and some had to make do with the Jagdpanther's 88mm PaK 43/3. The tank's machine-gun in the hull front was retained and a grenade launcher was also fitted to deter stalkers.

The Jagdtiger weighed around 71 tons, more than any other AFV that has ever seen widespread service in any army, and was seriously underpowered. Reliability was also poor since it used the same engine and drive train that was used in the King Tiger. The Jagdtiger equipped independent tank destroyer battalions, usually those of the Waffen SS.

Weight 70.6 tons (71.7 tonnes)
Crew six
Armament
One 128-mm PaK 80 (Li55) gun with 38 rounds and
One MG 34 machine-gun with 2,925 rounds
Armour
hull nose 100 mm, glacis 150 mm, sides and tail 80 mm, decking 40 mm;
superstructure front 250 mm. sides and rear 80 mm, top 40 mm
Engine one Maybach HL 230 P 30 V-121iquid-cooled petrol, 600hp
Speed 23.6 mph (38 km/h)
Range 68.4 miles (110 km)
Trench crossing 8 feet 2 inches (2.5 m)
Vertical step 2 feet 9.5 inches (85 cm)
Fording 5 feet 3 inches (1.6 m)
Overall length 35 feet (10.66 m)
Width wide tracks: 12 ft 3.5 ins (4. 72 m), narrow tracks 10 ft 8 ins (3.27 m)
Height 9 feet 3 inches (2.82 m)

Panzerjäger RSO

Introduced in 1944, typical of many late-war improvised gun carriages was the Panzerjager RSO, a light tank destroyer. This replaced the normal cab with a very low, armoured, structure. A 75mm PaK40 anti-tank gun minus its carriage was mounted on the flat bed of the cargo body. The PzJg RSO was mechanically identical to the standard vehicle, 83 examples were produced.

Panzerjager RSO
Crew 4
Weight 3.5tons
Armament
One 75mm Pak 40
Length 14ft 6ins
Width 6ft 6.5ins
Power plant Steyr 1500A petrol engine, producing 70hp

STURMGESCHUTZ III

The development of the StuG III was started in 1936 when the Heereswaffenamt agreed to a request from the Inspector of infantry's department for an armoured vehicle to provide fire support for the infantry.

Daimler Benz were instructed to prepare designs based on the PzKpfwIII, and Krupp were to develop the superstructure and armament. The new design was based on the PzKpfw III Ausf E chassis with a new, low, fully enclosed, armoured superstructure in which was mounted a 75mm L/24 gun.

A preproduction batch of thirty vehicles was ordered in 1939, followed by the first production model, the StuG III Ausf A, this was based on the chassis of the PzKpfw III Ausf F.

The end of 1940 saw the introduction the StuG III Ausf B, built on the new chassis of the PzKpfwIII Ausf H. The C and D incorporated only minor changes and the Ausf E was a command vehicle, provided with additional radio equipment

In September 1941 some vehicles were fitted with the more powerful 75mm L/33.

Crew 4
Weight 23.9 tons
Power plant one Maybach HL 120TRM engine, producing 300bhp
Maximum speed 25mph.
Armament
One 75mm StuK 40 L/48 gun
One 7.92mm MG43 machine gun.
Armour
Nose 80mm, driver's plate 30-50mm, sides and tail 30mm, decking 11-17 mm, belly 16mm
Length 22ft 2.5ins
Width 9ft 8.5ins
Height 7ft 1.25ins.

STURMPANZER IV BRUMMBAR

The Brummbar was developed as a result of experience in the heavy street fighting in Russia in 1941-2. Existing tanks and armoured assault guns had insufficient high-explosive capability to deal with fortified buildings, and existing heavy howitzers were too lightly protected. To overcome this problem a much more heavily armoured mounting for the 150mm SIG 33 heavy infantry gun was designed, based on the PzKpfw IV chassis. The vehicles were ordered in October 1942 and in service by April of the following year as the Sturmpanzer IV Brummbar (Grizzly Bear). Early Brummbars were based on the Ausf F and Ausf G chassis and had a relatively high armoured superstructure with 100mm sloping plates at the front and 70mm protection at the sides, with a new version of the infantry gun the SturmHaubitze 43 L/ 12 in a ball mounting in the front plate. Later models on the H and J chassis had several differences, including a modified gun mounting with a longer collar, a new driver's compartment with periscopes and eventually a new roomier superstructure with a machine-gun, lack of which had proved a serious weakness.

Weight 27.7 tons (28.2 tonnes)
Crew five
Armament
One 150mm StuH 43 (L/12) howitzer with 38 rounds
Armour
hull nose 80 mm, sides 30 mm, decking and tail 20 mm, belly 10 mm; superstructure front 100 mm, sides 30-70 mm, top 20 mm, rear 20-60 mm
Engine one Maybach HL 120 TRM V-12 water-cooled petrol, 300hp Speed 24 mph (38 km/h)
Trench crossing 7 feet 3 inches (2.2 m)
Fording 3 feet 1.5 inches (95 cm)
Overall length 19 feet 4.5 inches (5.91 m)
Width 9 feet 7 inches (2.92 m)
Height 8 feet (2.44 m)

STURMPANZER VI STURMTIGER

The Sturmtiger also known as the Sturmpanzer VI, was developed to fulfil requirements from the German Army engaged in the heavy street fighting at Stalingrad and other similar places in Russia. The full designation was 380mm RW 61 Auf StuMrs Tiger (380mm rocket projector Type 61 on Tiger chassis). When development work started on the project, it was decided that the then-new PzKpfw VI Tiger Ausf E chassis would be used. It was intended to mount a 210mm gun; but as no suitable weapon was available, it was proposed to use the Raketenwerfer 61 L/54, a German Navy antisubmarine weapon.

A model of the Sturmtiger was first shown on 20 October 1943, and the type went into limited production in August 1944, when the firm of Alkett converted ten existing Tiger tanks. For their intended role as mobile assault howitzers against troop concentrations and fortifications, they were heavily armoured. The suspension, power train, engine and hull were those of the basic Tiger E; but a heavy rectangular superstructure made of welded, rolled armour plates replaced the turret of the tank.

Crew five or six
Weight 66,9tons (68tonnes)
Power plant Maybach HL 210 engine of 694hp
Maximum road speed of 23mph
Armament
One 380mm Raketenwerfer 61 with 12 rounds
One 7.92mm MG 34 machine-gun
Armour
Superstructure front 150mm, sides and rear 84mm, top 40mm
Hull nose 100mm, glacis 60mm, driver's plate 100mm, sides 60-80mm, decking and belly 26mm, tail 82mm
Overall length 20ft 8.5ins (6.30m)
Width 12ft 3ins (on combat tracks) narrow tracks: 10 feet 4 inches (3.15 m)
Height (with crane) 11ft 4ins (3.45m)
Trench crossing 7 feet 6 inches (2.29m)
Vertical step 2 feet 7 inches (79cm)
Fording 4 feet (1.22 m)

150mm Sig33 auf PzKpfw III Bison

From December 1941 to October 1942 a small batch of 24 PzKpfw III Ausf H tanks, chassis numbers 90751-91036 and 91401-91750, were converted to take the infantry 15cm sIG33 gun, housed in a closed box in place of the normal turret. Unlike earlier attempts to mount the 15cm Sig33 in a self-propelled chassis, this vehicle consisted of a fully enclosed box type armoured superstructure with a short 15cm howitzer mounted in the front plate, offset to the right of the vehicle's centre line. An MG 34 was also mounted in the front plate. In the superstructure roof was a hatch and a large ventilator fan. The Sturminfanteriegeschutz 33B saw service in Russia.

Crew 5
Weight 21tons
Engine Maybach HL120TRM producing 300hp
Speed 40km/h (24.8mph)
Range 110km (68.35miles)
Length: 5.4m (17ft 8.5ins)
Width: 2.9m (9ft 6ins)
Height: 2.3m (7ft 6ins)
Armament
One 15cm StuIG L/11 with 30 rounds
One 7.92rnm MG 34 with 600 rounds.
Armour front 50mm + 30mm, side 50mm.

SDKTZ 124 WESPE 105MM

The most numerous SP on the PzKpfw II chassis was the Wespe (Wasp SdKfz 124). This mounted a 105mm leFH 18/2 field howitzer in a high superstructure at the rear of the hull. The engine was moved forward to the centre of the chassis and the driver remained at the front. The howitzer could traverse 11° either side of centre and elevate from -15° to +42°, this relatively high elevation for an SP mount gave a range of 10,500 metres. The Wespe could carry 32 105mm rounds and was usually accompanied by unarmed Wespes acting as ammunition carriers. Some 682 were converted during 1943 and 1944, mostly by Famo in Warsaw and they saw wide spread service in the self-propelled artillery battalions of the Panzer and Panzer Grenadier divisions.

Weight 11.5tons (12.1 tonnes)
Crew five
Armament
one 105mm le FH 18/2 (L/28) field howitzer with 32 rounds
one 7.92-mm MG 34 machine-gun with 600 rounds
Armour hull nose and driver's plate, glacis 10 mm, sides 15 mm, decking 10 mm, belly 5 mm, rear 8-15 mm; superstructure front 12 mm. sides 10 mm, rear 8 mm
Range 90 miles
Height 7 feet 8 inches (2.32 m)
Other details as PzKpfw 1I Ausf F tank

600mm Morsar Karl (Gerat 040)

The largest tracked vehicles of all were the huge 600mm mortars, which were projected before the war. These might best be described as motorised tracked gun carriages. They were not Panzer Division vehicles and were in fact classified as siege artillery, but were actually self-propelled carriages with driving compartments. The first vehicle was built by Rheinmetall-Borsig in 1939, under the designation 600mm Morser Karl (Gerat 040), and was intended to bombard the massively defended forts of the Maginot Line on the Franco-German border. The vehicle weighed 120tonnes, was 11.15 metres long, and had 12-mm armour plate. The vehicle had a top speed of 6 mph. A second vehicle was built, designated 600mm Morser Karl II. By the time the two vehicles were in service France had fallen. Named Thor and Eva, the two pieces saw service on the Eastern Front and were particularly successful in the siege of Sevastopol in 1942, and also at Brest-Litovsk.

In 1943, as a result of these operations, six improved vehicles were ordered, designated 540mm Morser Karl (Gerat 041). The mortar was of different calibre, but it was generally similar to the original vehicle and weighed 130 tonnes.

Length: 36.58 ft
Width: 10.33 ft
Weight: 264,455 lb
Speed: 6 mph
Armour: 15 mm
Armament: 600mm 040 mortar

FLAKPANZER IV MOBELWAGEN

This was an extemporised AA vehicle on the chassis of the Panzer IV. It consisted of an AA gun complete with mount fixed to a platform mounted over the turret ring of the base vehicle. The thin armoured shields had to be dropped down to provide a clear field of fire. Thus leaving the crew largely un-protected. It was replaced by the much better Wirbelwind.

The Wirbelwind first appeared in December 1943 and was a great improvement over the previous Mobelwagen type AA vehicle. The Flakvierling weapon was mounted in a 16mm armoured revolving open-topped turret that provided the gun crew with all round protection. The Wirbelwind (Whirlwind) and was built by Ostbau using a PzKpfw IV Ausf J chassis. From March 1944 it was supplemented by the Ostwind (East Wind), built by Deutsche Eisenwerke, which mounted the 37mm FlaK 43 in a heavier, 25mm armoured turret. The rates of fire of these weapons were respectively 800 to 1,800 rounds per minute and 80 to 160 rounds. Some 140 Wirbelwind and 40 Ostwind vehicles were built but they could not do a great deal to mitigate the effects of Allied air power.

Crew 5
Armament
four 20-mm Flakvierling 38s with 3,200 rounds,
one hull machine-gun with 1,350 rounds
Armour
hull nose and drivers plate 80 mm, glacis 20 mm, sides 30 mm, belly 10-20 mm, tail 20 mm;
Turret sides 16mm.
Engine one Maybach HL 120 TRM V-12 water-cooled petrol, 300hp
Speed 26 mph (42 km/h)
Range 125 miles (200 km)
Trench crossing 7 feet 7 inches (23 m)
Vertical step 2 feet (60 cm)
Fording 2 feet 7.5 inches (80 cm)
Overall length 19 feet 4.5 inches (5.91 m)
Width 9 feet 7 inches (2.92 m)

Sdkfz 234/4 (late model 8 wheeled armoured car with 75mm PAK 40)

It was August 1940 when work started on a replacement for the original eight-wheeled armoured cars. Bussing-NAG undertook design and construction, while Deutschen produced the hull, which was similar to that of the preceding series of eight-wheelers, but was much simplified. New one-piece mudguards with integral stowage boxes replaced the two separate groups of mudguards that covered the wheels on the earlier models.

A prime requirement for the new design was that it should operate well at extremes of climate, particularly in tropical climates. The Czech firm of Tatra was given the task of developing a high-powered engine to replace the original engine, and a compact V-12 14.8 litre unit was evolved.

The prototype did not appear until July 1941, by which time German troops were fighting in North Africa, and the complicated Tatra engine proved too noisy for desert operations. It was rejected and an improved engine designed with the major aim of muffing the noise. Externally the new vehicle appeared similar to the original Bussing-NAG design, but one major difference was that it had a monocoque hull instead of a separate chassis.

Heavy Armoured Car
Length 22.3f t (inc gun)
Width 7.64ft
Weight 25,880lb
Speed 53 mph
Range early model 500 miles, late model 620 miles
Armour
Turret 40mm max, 100mm on mantlet
Hull front 30mm, side 14mm, all other plates 10mm
Armament
One 50mm KwK39/1
One 7.92-mm MG 42

Sdkfz 251 Ausf D

The Sdkfz251 was designed as an APC and basically consists of an armoured body mounted on the chassis of the 3ton half track built by Hanomag (Hannoverische Maschinenbau AG), as this was the most suitably sized vehicle to transport a complete infantry section or squad of ten men. After exploring several alternative layouts, it was decided to use a front-engined chassis, mounting a body with an open-topped rear compartment and rear doors. This would enable troops to disembark over the sides or through the rear doors and offered the additional benefit of using the 3ton Sdkfz11 chassis virtually unchanged.

Work on the armoured personnel carrier began in 1937. Minor changes to the chassis were made and an armoured body was produced by Bussing-NAG. The body was of a faceted well-sloped design, heavily influenced by German armoured cars of the time, to maximise the effectiveness of the armour. The prototype was ready in 1938 and, after successful trials, the vehicle was rushed into production.

The first production vehicles entered service in the spring of 1939 and went to equip an infantry company in I Panzer Division for troop trials, which proved to be a great success.

Power plant Maybach HL 42 engine producing 100hp,
Maximum speed of 34mph.
Range 300km (186miles)
Armour front 14.5mm, sides and rear 8mm
Armament
Two 7.92mm machine-guns
Length 19ft 2.5ins
Width 6ft 10.5ins
Height 5ft 10ins
Weight is 17,182lb.
Fording 6.6m (2ft)
Vertical obstacle 2.0m (6ft 6.7in)

Sdkfz 251/1 with Wurfkorper rockets (usually 5 x 280mm HE and 1 x 320mm Incendiary)

Highly successful in its own right the SdKfz 251/1 APC also served as the basis of a whole range of special purpose vehicles, these are listed below.

Wurfkorper

One important variant that did not receive an ordnance number consisted of racks mounting three Wurfkorper MFl 50 rockets on either side of a standard SdKfz 251. The rockets could be either the 28cm incendiary or 32cm HE or a mixture of both and had range of 2,028m. The rockets were highly inaccurate and aiming was achieved by simply pointing the vehicle in the general direction of the target, so they tended to be used en masse where possible.

SdKfz 251/2.

This was adapted as an 80mm mortar carrier for the heavy support companies. Some of the seating was removed to provide stowage for mortar rounds, the mortar could be fired from the vehicle but was fired from cover, on the ground whenever possible.

SdKfz 251/3

A radio vehicle and was fitted with a variety of radio equipment depending on its specific role.

SdKfz 251/4

Was an artillery tractor. Fitted with racks for ammunition stowage it was used to tow the artillery pieces of the armoured divisions, including the 105mm Leichte Feldhaubittze, the 50mm PaK 38 and the 75mm PaK 40.

SdKfz 251/5 and 251/7

Both engineers' vehicles. The 251/5 carried the assault engineers of an armoured battalion with their inflatable boats and assault bridges. The 251/7 or Pioneerpanzerwagen had brackets on the superstructure sides to carry bridging ramps and also carried inflatable assault boats and demolition charges.

SdKfz 251/6

Known as the Kommandopanzerwagen was a command vehicle and was suitably equipped with radio gear, map tables and cipher machines. The

SdKfz 251/8

An armoured ambulance.

SdKfz 251/10

Mounted a 37mm PaK 36 in place of the forward machine gun.

SDKFZ251/9 (75MM KWK L24)

251/10

Usually issued to platoon leaders and were used to give covering fire to other vehicles in the group. It entered service in 1940.

SdKfz 251/9

It mounted the short-barrelled 75mm KwK L24 used in early versions of the Panzer IV and was usually issued on the basis of one, six vehicle company, per battalion of the Panzer Grenadiers.

SdKfz 251/11

Telephone cable layer.

SdKfz 251/12, 251/13, 251/14 and 251/15

All specialist artillery vehicles used for roles such as surveying, range finding and flash spotting. They were used by assault gun and artillery units of the Panzer Divisions.

SdKfz 251/16

Flamethrower vehicle, it mounted one flame projector each side of the superstructure and sometimes carried a third on an extension hose for use outside the vehicle.

SdKfz 251/17

Introduced in 1942 and mounted either a 20mm FlaK 30 or FlaK 38 in the rear compartment. There were several variations in the mounting.

SdKfz 251/18

An armoured observation vehicle.

SdKfz 251/19

A telephone exchange vehicle, used by communication units.

Sdkfz251/20

Uhu (owl) was an infrared searchlight vehicle, used in conjunction with Panther tanks equipped with infrared searchlights and sensors.

SdKfz 251/21

Fitted with the 15mm Drilling MG 151 triple machine gun mount, an obsolete Luftwaffe weapon to produce a cheap and effective defence against air attack.

SdKfz 251/22

The 75mm PaK 40 anti-tank gun, minus its carriage, was fitted into the fighting compartment of the half-track to produce a surprisingly effective self-propelled gun.

SDKFZ 250 ALTE

The SdKfz 250 resulted from a decision, in 1939, to build an armoured version of the Demag D7 SdKfz 10. An armoured prototype of the larger SdKfz 11, the SdKfz 251 had already been built and successfully tested, and it was felt that a smaller vehicle would be useful for some tasks.

The first obstacle to the design of the new vehicle was that the chassis of the D7 was designed around a Maybach HL 42 engine that produced only 100hp. While this was perfectly adequate for the un-armoured vehicle it was felt that the weight of an armoured body would degrade the vehicle's performance to an unacceptable degree. To overcome this problem it was decided to shorten the rear suspension by one road wheel, and to reduce the length of the chassis, thus permitting the fitting of a shorter, and therefore lighter, armoured body.

Bussing-NAG, who had produced the armoured body for the Sdkfz251, were commissioned to design a body for the new vehicle, and this was fitted to a prototype chassis provided by Demag. The new half-track performed well in tests and was immediately ordered into production. The Demag offered a slightly inferior performance to the SdKfz 251 and, of course,

had a less capacious body, but it was able to take on many of the functions previously undertaken by the Sdkfz251, thus freeing it up for tasks that required a larger vehicle.

The Sdkfz250 first saw action in 1940 in the invasion of France and was soon being adapted for a multitude of special roles. In all, the armoured 1ton half-track was produced in 14 officially recognised variants as well as numerous ad hoc field modifications.

In 1943 a programme of rationalisation was put in hand to improve the efficiency of war production. To this end the design of many vehicles was to be simplified, and in the case of the Sdkfz250 this was to lead a major redesign of the armoured body. The original production hull was of a complicated multifaceted shape that was bowed-out in the middle to increase interior space. The new design reduced the number of plates used in construction by almost half. The front and rear were now made of single plates, side stowage lockers were integral to the hull, the side vision flaps were replaced with slits, all mudguards were made of flat sheet steel and the vehicle was provided with a single headlight. In this form the 250 was to remain in production until

1944 and remained in service until the end of the war in Europe. On the introduction of the new, simplified, vehicle the suffix alt for alter Art (original model) was added to the designation of original production vehicles whilst the new vehicle was known as the Sdkfz250 neu or neuer Art (new).

Crew 6
Power plant Maybach HL 42 engine producing 100 hp,
Maximum speed of 37mph
Weight 5.3tons (1ton of which was the payload)
Armour front 14.5mm, sides and rear 8mm.
Length 15ft
Width 6ft 2.5ins
Height 6ft 3ins.

SDKFZ 250/5 NEU; SDKFZ 250/9 (SDKFZ222 TURRET)

The SdKfz 250

Served as the basis for a whole host of variants these are listed below.

Sdkfz250/1.

This was a plain armoured personnel carrier and was mainly used by platoon or company commanders. It was usually fitted with two swivel mounted machine guns and could carry six men

Sdkfz250/2

A telephone line layer, which was also used as an observation vehicle.

SdKfz 250 /3, /4 and /5

Were all radio vehicles, and differed only in their radio equipment, depending on their role. Early SdKfz 250/3s had the characteristic bedstead frame aerial but this was replaced with a simpler pole aerial in later vehicles. All three radio vehicles looked externally similar to the basic vehicle with their aerials dismantled.

SdKfz 250/6

An ammunition carrier for the replenishment of assault guns. It was fitted with one of two arrangements of racks, either for 70 rounds for the short-barrelled 75mm gun or 60 rounds of long barrelled 75mm ammunition. This version replaced the SdKfz 252, in service. The SdKfz 252 had a different body shape to the 250, having the rear of the body cut down to save weight and being totally enclosed with an armoured roof.

SdKfz 250/7

Mortar vehicle that carried the 80mm mortar. The mortar could be fired from the vehicle but was dismounted and fired from the ground whenever possible. The 250/7 largely replaced the SdKfz 251 in this role, as the 3ton half-track was overly large for the task.

SdKfz 250/8

Armed with the redundant short 75mm KwK 37 L24 guns from up-gunned PzIVs to provide the motorised infantry with their own fire support. In service the SdKfz 250/8 proved to be fully interchangeable with the larger, similarly armed, Hanomag SdKfz 251/9.

SdKfz 250/9

Produced to increase the mobility of reconnaissance units on the Eastern Front who were finding the mobility of their armoured cars severely restricted by the heavy Russian mud.

SCHWERER WERMACHTSCHLEPPER WITH 150MM PANZERWERFER 42

In 1941, the German Army decided to replace its range of five different un-armoured half-track chassis with two standardised designs. The first of the two the Leichter Wehrmachtschlepper or light army tractor never progressed beyond the prototype stage, but the Schwerer Wehrmachtschlepper, or army heavy tractor, was much more succesful. To keep costs down and ease production the bodywork was much simpler than previous half-tracks, consisting of an open cab and a flat bed body with steel mesh drop-sides; and the complex roller needle bearing tracks gave way to a simpler dry pin type. Production was slow, partly due to the lack of priority accorded the vehicle and partly due to the attentions of RAF Bomber Command. However, production continued until the end of the World War II, with a few vehicles seeing service in the post-war Czech Army. Variants included an anti-aircraft vehicle mounting a FlaK 43 37mm gun on an open platform, and a frontline supply vehicle both with armoured cabs; and a fully armoured version mounting the ten-barrelled 150mm Panzerwerfer 42 rocket launcher.

Crew 2
Weight 13,500kg (29,700lb)
Length 6.68m (21ft 11in)
Width 2.50m (8ft 24in)
Height 2.83m (9ft 3.4in)
Range 300km (187 miles)
Armour 8-15mm (0.31-0.59in)
Armament see text
Power plant one Maybach HL 42 six-cylinder petrol engine developing 100hp (74.6kW)
Performance maximum road speed 27km/h (16.8mph)
Fording 0.6m (2ft)

SDKFZ 7/2 37MM FLAK 36

Development of the SdKfz 7 can be traced back to a 1934 requirement for an eight-tonne (7.87 tons) half-track. The vehicle first appeared in 1938 and was destined to be used mainly as the tractor for the 8.8cm flak guns. The vehicle could carry up to 12 men and a considerable quantity of supplies, as well as pulling a load of up to 8000kg (17,600Ib). Most were fitted with a winch, and the vehicle was successful in service and popular with troops. There were several variants including a fire control vehicle for the V2 rocket and a flat bed load carrier. Two anti-aircraft versions were built the SdKfz 7/1 and the SdKfz 7/2; the first mounting the quad 2cm Flakveirling and the second 3.7cm FlaK36, both versions were made with and without armoured cabs and bonnets. Close copies of the SdKfz 7 were produced by Fiat and Breda in Italy and a prototype of a very similar vehicle was even built by Bedford in the UK although it was not put into production.

Crew 12
Weight 11,550kg (25,410lb)
Length 6.85m (20ft 3in)
Width 2.40m (7ft 10.5in)
Height 262m (8ft 7.1in)
Range 250km (156 miles)
Armour basic version - none
Armament basic version - none
Power plant one Maybach HL 62 six-cylinder petrol engine developing 140hp (104.4kW)
Performance maximum road speed 50km/h (31 mph); fording 05m (lft 7in); vertical obstacle 20m (61t 6 7in)

SdKfz9, 18ton half-track Famo F3

The largest of the German wartime half-tracks, the SdKfz 9 (FAMO F3 model) or Schwerer Zugkraftwagen 18t was introduced in 1939. It was the third in a series of 18ton vehicles developed by FAMO, the first two being the FMgr1 and F2 of 1936 and 38 respectively. Succeeding the F2 in 1939, the F3 was in most respects similar but for it's more powerful Maybach HL 108 TUKRM V12 engine which produced 250bhp and which was also fitted in the PzKpfw IV. It was used primarily as a vehicle to recover tanks and to tow the 24ton trailers on which damaged tanks were transported to base workshops.

The FAMO was not powerful enough to tow heavier tanks such as the Tiger and Panther, then entering service, but it was retained in the recovery role for the Panzer IV and various assault guns. Until the introduction of the Bergepanther armoured recover vehicle, the half-tracks were used in multiples, linked in tandem, for the recovery of Tigers and Panthers. At about this time some vehicles were fitted with a large earth spade to assist in winching out heavy tanks.

Crew 9
Weight 18tons
Maximum speed 31mph
Length 27ft 1in
Width 8ft 6ins
Height 9ft 1in.

SDKFZ10, 1TON HALF-TRACK DEMAG D7

The Demag D7 was the product of a five-year development programme that culminated in the preproduction model, the D6, in 1937. The following year the design was finalised and the first production model, the D7, entered service. The D7 remained in production, virtually unchanged, until 1944.

The Sdkfz10's good cross-country performance and 1.5ton payload led to it being adopted for a number of specialised roles. These included a gas detector vehicle and decontamination unit. The Demag was also used as a self propelled mount for light anti-aircraft guns and for anti-tank guns. The light AA vehicle SdKfz 10/4 mounted a 2cm Flak 30 on a flat bed body with steel mesh fold down sides. The later model SdKfz 10/5 mounted the 2cm Flak38, which offered an increase in the rate of fire from 120 to 220, rounds a minute. From 1941 onwards the light AA vehicles were often fitted with an armoured cab and the gun itself was generally fitted with a shield. Since ammunition stowage on the vehicle was limited, a single axle ammunition trailer was sometimes provided to carry additional rounds.

Crew 8
Power plant Maybach HL 38 or 42 TKRM 6cyl petrol engine, producing 100bhp
Maximum speed 40mph
Weight 4.9 tons
Towing capacity 1ton.
Length 15ft 7ins
Width 6ft
Height 5ft 4ins
Fording 0.75m (29.5in)

SDKFZ2 KLEINES KETTENKRAFTRAD HALFTRACK MOTORBIKE

The Kliene Kettenkraftrad or Kettenkrad was unique in being a half-track motorcycle. It was originally developed for use as a tractor to tow the light guns of the Para troop and airborne units. With this in mind the vehicle's design was such that it could be transported in a Junkers Ju52 3m aircraft, the standard transport plane of the Luftwaffe.

The Kettenkrad was fitted with motorcycle type front forks and it's tracks were a scaled-down version of those found on the larger half-tracks. The driver was provided with a motorcycle type saddle and two passengers could be accommodated on a rear-facing bench seat. Entering service in 1941, the Kettenkrad first saw action in the airborne landing on Crete, where it was used to transport supplies and ammunition, and to tow light artillery pieces. It remained in use with the Luftwaffe's airborne troops until the end of the War, and also served with the army, seeing action in North Africa, the Eastern Front, NW Europe and Italy.

Crew 3
Engine 1.5litre Opel Olympia38, 4cylinder, water-cooled petrol, producing 36bhp.
Maximum speed 50mph
Maximum towed load 0.45ton
Weight 1.2 tons.
Length 9ft
Width 3ft 3ins
Height 3ft 4ins.

STEYR RSO/01

The Steyr RSO or Raupenschlepper-Ost (tracked tractor East) was designed specifically to deal with the atrocious conditions on the Eastern front. In the summer the roads were dusty, rutted, sun-baked tracks, in the autumn rain and spring thaw they were transformed in to a morass, and in the Winter they would be frozen hard and covered in several feet of snow.

The vehicle produced by Steyr was in effect a fully tracked truck and was intended to perform the same roles. It was fitted with a pressed-steel truck-type cab and was fitted with a drop side cargo body at the rear. The payload was 1.5 metric tons. For winter operations the vehicle was provided with wider, 600mm, snow tracks, but most photographs show the RSO fitted with the standard 340mm ones. In 1944 a simplified model, the RSO/03 was introduced. Built by Magirus, it had a flat panel open-top cab with a canvas hood and was powered by a Magirus engine, by the last year of the war RSOs were also being used in the West.

Crew 1
Weight 3.5tons
Payload 1.5tons
Length 14ft 6ins
Width 6ft 6.5ins
Height 8ft 3.5ins
Power plant Steyr 1500A petrol engine, producing 70hp

Mercedes 170V staff car

The Mercedes 170V was the culmination of a series of Daimler-Benz passenger cars dating back to 1931. Introduced in1935 it featured a new tubular chassis that owed much to the Type 130H series of rear-engined cars. Not only were tubes used instead of box-section pressed members but they were laid out in the form of a backbone down the centre of the car. The by-now traditional Daimler-Benz independent suspensions were also specified, with transverse leaf springs at the front and coil springs and swing axles at the rear. The front mounted 1.7litre side-valve four-cylinder engine was also taken from the rear-engined 170H. The styling of the new car was restrained, but unmistakably Daimler-Benz. It was available with several different Sindelfingen built separate bodies, including delivery vehicles and ambulances. Models built for military use included hard top and convertible touring bodies as staff cars, and, under the Einheits Program, Kfz1 Kubelsitzer field cars and Kfz2 and Kfz2/40 fitted out for signals and small repairs respectively. More than 90,000 examples were built before production was suspended at the end of 1942 and production was resumed after the end of the War, continuing until the early 1950s.

Power plant 1.7 litre four-cylinder Mercedes Benz engine, producing 38bhp
Maximum speed 67mph.
Length 14ft
Width 5ft 2ins
Height 5ft 1.5ins
Weight 1.08 tons.

VOLKSWAGEN TYPE 82 KUBELWAGEN

The origins of the Kubelwagen lie with a design for a lightweight, affordable car created by Dr Ferdinand Porsche in the early 30s. Several prototypes were followed by the 30 strong Series 30 pre production batch and then 44 examples of the Series 38 model, which were subjected to a total of over 1,500,000 miles of road testing. The KdF was a small, streamlined, four-seater, sedan and after the war would become the most extensively produced car ever under the more familiar name of the Beetle. The intention was to produce the KdF-Wagen, as the production car was known, at a rate of over a million units a year and to this end a gigantic new production plant was constructed. Complete with it's own power station and a new town for the workers, it was sited on the banks of the Mitteland Canal at the village of Fallersleben, part of the 14th century estate of Schloss Wolfsburg. The majority of the plant had been completed by early 1939 and production of the KdF (Kraft durch Freude - Strength Through Joy) had reached a total of just 210 vehicles when Germany went to war. Production of the KdF-Wagen continued on a limited basis throughout the war reaching a total of 630 vehicles by the war's end. The majority of the new Wolfsburg plant's wartime

production was to take another form however. In 1939 Porsche was asked to develop a militarised version of the KdF for use by the Wermacht, for although the armoured divisions were well equipped, a new, simpler and more easily produced replacement for the Stoewer 40 light field car was called for as part of the Schell-Programm of transport rationalisation. The job of developing the new vehicle fell to Ferdinand Porsche's son, Ferry.

The new vehicle known as the Type 82 or Type 2 Kubelwagen (Bucket-Car) used the running gear and floor pan of the Kdf with a modification to the suspension to increase ground clearance. Early production Kubels used the same 985cc 22.5hp engine as the KdF but in March 1943 a change was made to a 1131cc 25hp unit. The body was open topped, constructed from ribbed, flat panels and was produced by Ambi-Budd in Berlin. The design was ready for approval by December 1939 and prototypes were sent to Poland for field trials with the Panzer divisions. These proved to be a great success and production commenced in March 1941, a few examples entering service in time for the invasions of France and the Low Countries. The Kubelwagen

was popular in service, soon dispelling fears that it's lack of four wheel drive would make it a poor cross country vehicle. Indeed in the Western Desert it was generally held to perform better on sand than the four wheel drive Jeep, and on the Eastern front it's light weight enabled it to keep going in the heavy Russian mud when most other vehicles were bogged down. The Kubel was used by all branches of the German armed forces, Luftwaffe, Navy, Wermacht and Waffen SS. It's roles included light reconnaissance, staff car, light transport, ambulance and assault engineer carrier and production was to total over 50,000.

Power plant 985cc, 22.5hp, 4-cylinder, air cooled engine until March 1943, later vehicles 1131cc, 25hp unit
Length 12ft 3ins
Width 5ft 3ins
Height 5ft 6ins with the roof raised
Weight 1,470lbs
Maximum speed 50mph
Fording 0.4m (1ft 4ins)

SCHWIMMWAGEN

The Schwimmwagen was a development of the Type 82 Kubelwagen, and was initially intended for use on the Eastern Front where the poor roads and numerous waterways made a vehicle with amphibious capabilities particularly desirable, although the Schwimmwagen was, in the event, also used extensively in the West. Mechanically the new vehicle was similar to the Kubel, but it employed four wheel drive instead of the earlier vehicle's two wheel drive. The body was completely new and was basically a watertight, welded steel tub that provided the necessary buoyancy. The vehicle was propelled in the water by a three bladed propeller mounted on a stub shaft on a swing arm at the rear of the body, which was raised and lowered by a simple push rod. When the propeller was hinged down into position the stub shaft engaged a dog clutch on the camshaft of the rear mounted engine. Steering in the water was achieved by turning the front wheels. Early Schwimmwagens, the Type 128, were fitted with the 984cc engine and only 150 of these were built, by Porsche in 1940, for field trials. All subsequent models came fitted with the more powerful 1131cc, 25hp engine, as the German Waffenamt (Weapons Department) had, by this time,

set 25hp as the basic minimum military requirement. The Type 138 followed and eventually the Type 166. This was the major production version of the Schwimmwagen and, with a shortened wheelbase and reduced weight leading to an overall improvement in performance, it soon became the most sought after model. The majority of Type 166s went to the SS as they were given preferential treatment in the allocation of equipment.

By the War's end 14,238 Schwimmwagens of all types had been constructed, the majority at Volkswagen's Wolfsburg plant with some being produced at Porche's facility.

Power plant 1131cc air-cooled engine producing 25 horsepower
Maximum speed of 6mph in the water and 50 mph on land.
Armament
One 7.92mm machine gun sometimes fitted
Length 12ft 7.75ins
Width 4ft 10.5ins
Height (with hood erected) 5ft 3.5ins

AUTO-UNION/HORCH KFZ70

As part of the 1934 Einheits rationalisation programme Auto-Union/Horch were selected as producers of both the medium and heavy chassis. The Auto-Union/Horch Chassis I for heavy passenger cars was produced in 1935. As part of the programme, it was also intended to use the chassis for armoured cars, in a rear-engined form and this became known as the SdKfz 221, 222 and 223 Series.

Initially all production was taken up by armoured car production since this was the most pressing need, and production of passenger cars did not begin until 1938. The front-engined chassis for passenger cars was designated Chassis II and early vehicles were fitted with four wheel steering, but from 1940 onwards this was omitted. At about this time the Berlin Ford factory also became engaged in production, Ford built vehicles were externally similar but were fitted with a Ford 3.6 litre V8 78hp engine in place of the Horch unit. A novel feature of early vehicles was the provision of a recess either side of the body in which the spare wheels were free to rotate on stub axles mounted on the chassis. Production ceased in 1941 when, due to further rationalisation under the Schnell-Programme, it was decided that

all heavy passenger cars would share the chassis of the 1.5ton light truck. However, the Auto Union/Horch heavy cars remained in service and were widely used on all fronts until the end of the War.

The heavy passenger car was also used as the basis of several special purpose vehicles, some of which utilised the standard body but with alterations in equipment and stowage such as the Kfz13 Telephone Truck, Kfz83 Light Searchlight Truck, Kfz59 Light Gun Tractor and Kfz81 Light AA Vehicle, and some that were fitted with a closed van type body such as the Kfz31 Ambulance and the Kfz24 Maintenance Truck.

The Auto Union/Horch Kfz 70 was fitted with an Auto Union/Horch 81 bhp 3,823cc V8 engine, a crew of six including the driver and its dimensions are:- length, 15ft 11ins; width, 6ft 6.75ins; height, 6ft 8.25ins.Specs

Kfz 1 light field car BWM 40; Kfz 2 Stoewer

Kfz 1 was the ordnance number given to light passenger cars under the system introduced in 1933, when Hitler came to power and the Reichswehr was transformed into the modern Wermacht. In 1934 the Einheits (or Standard) Programme was instigated. This aimed to develop replacements for the various transport vehicles in service that would be designed specifically for military use. There were to be a limited number of suppliers for each class of vehicle, and the vehicle was to be produced to a standard design regardless of the manufacturer with the exception of the engine which would always be that of the manufacturer and commercially available. Although the design and layout of the vehicle should be such that the engines of other assigned makers could be fitted without major alterations.

In the case of the Kfz1 Light Standard Cross-Country Personnel Carrier the selected suppliers were Hanomag, BMW and Stoewer. BMW of Eisenach built the original version, designated L E Pkw/325 (Leichter Einheits Personenkraftwagen 325 or Light Standard Personnel Carrier 325), which was produced from 1937 to 1940. This was followed by the Hanomag model, the L E Pkw/20-B produced from 1937-40.

Engine Stoewer AW2 petrol, producing 50bhp
Weight 3,748lb
Length 12ft 7.5ins
Width 5ft 6.5ins
Height (with tilt erected) 6ft 3ins.

FORD V3000S 3 TON TRUCK

After the partial success of the Einheits programme of 1934 General Schell, Director of Motorisation for the Wermacht, instigated a further rationalisation plan in 1938. The specification laid down for the standard medium truck called for a four-wheeled truck, rated to carry 3 tons. The companies selected to produce the medium truck include Opel, Daimler-Benz, Magirus, Borgward and Ford, all of whom produced both A and S Type vehicles except Ford whom only produced 4x2s. Most manufacturers gave their vehicle in this class the designation 3000 (the payload in Kg) and so The Ford model became the Ford V3000 S.

The Fords were produced at various plants in occupied Europe and Germany including Antwerp, Amsterdam, Cologne and Poissy. They were essentially a 'Germanized' edition of the pre-war American 1 1/2ton 4x2, rated at 3 metric tonnes for military use. Various austerity measures were introduce in the course of production, many vehicles for example are fitted with flat section front mudguards and in 1944 the 'ersatz' cab known as the Wermacht-Eihhetsfahrerhaus was introduced.

Engine 3.9 litre V8 petrol, producing 95bhp
Max road speed 80km/ (50mph)
Range 410km (255miles)
Weight 3.29 tonnes (3.23tons)
Length 20ft 1.5ins
Width 7ft 4.5ins
Height 7ft 1.5ins
Capacity 3tonnes
Fording 05.m (1ft 7in)

OPEL BLITZ 3 TON TRUCK

The Opel Blitz was one of the most successful products of an attempt by the Germans to standardise their vehicle fleet (100 different vehicles were In service by the late 1930s, leading to massive logistical difficulties). The Blitz had a steel cab and wooden body and was used in many roles, from field ambulance to mobile workshop to command vehicle. To improve cross-country performance, some vehicles were produced with four-wheel drive, these vehicles being designated Allrad. They were used in all theatres of the war, with later models having cabs constructed of pressed card to conserve steel. Production lasted until 1944, when allied bombing and ground advances overtook the factories. The Blitz was well built, and was the most reliable of the German 3ton trucks in rugged conditions. In an attempt to improve the mobility of supply vehicles in the harsh terrain of the Eastern Front many were produced with the rear wheels replaced by light tank tracks and suspension in a conversion known as the Opel Maultier, or Mule. This proved so successful that similar modifications were also applied to several other types of truck.

Crew. 1
Weight: 3290kg (7238Ib)
Length 6.02m (19ft gin)
Width 2.265m (7ft 5.2in)
Height 2.175m (7ft 1.6in)
Range 410km (255 miles)
Armour: none
Armament: none
Power plant: one Opel six-cylinder petrol engine developing 73.5hp (548kW)
Maximum road speed 80km/h (50mph)
Fording 0.5m (1ft 7in)

BMW R12 COMBINATION—BMW R12 MOTORCYCLE; BMW R35 MOTORCYCLE; BMW R75 MOTORCYCLE

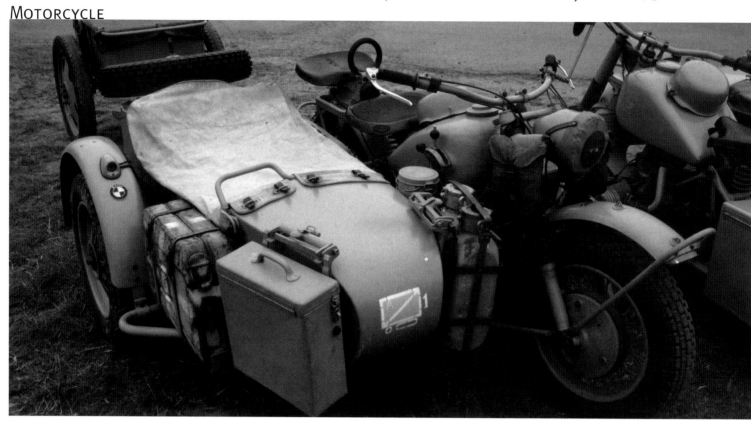

A commercial model impressed into military service, BMW started to produce the R12 motorcycle in 1935 and continued to manufacture them until the end of 1941. It was an instant hit with the motorcycling public throughout Germany and other European countries due to the fact that it had a robust, reliable engine and an exceptionally smooth ride due to it's oil filled hydraulic front forks.

The R12 was ideally suited to military service and the majority of the approximately 36,000 produced saw service during World War Two. Over 20,000 were produced as civilian models, but most of these were requisitioned by the military. The remaining 10,000 or so were produced to military specifications. The R12 was in service with the Wehrmacht throughout the war and in every theatre of operations.

There were subtle changes in the specification for military use. These were mainly the use of foot pegs instead of the civilian aluminium footboards; extra strengthening around the steering yolk and pressed steel rear foot rests rather than aluminium. The military machine was also provided with leather panniers and masked lighting.

Engine BMW 750cc, 4 stroke, 2 cylinder, flat twin producing 18 hp
Gearbox, 4 speed
Transmission shaft drive
Weight 408lb.

Goliath Demolition Vehicle

The Goliath was a small, unmanned demolition vehicle, developed by Zundapp, and was produced in two versions. The SdKfz 302 and the SdKfz 303. The first was powered by an electric motor and was directed by radio-control, the second was fitted with a small petrol engine and was remotely- controlled via a cable, paid out from the rear of the vehicle as it moved forward. Goliaths were used in action in Italy, NW Europe, and on the Eastern Front. They were usually directed against fixed fortifications but were also used against tanks on occasion. They could carry over 75kg of explosive and presented a very small target but against this they were slow, 12mph, and easily disabled when hit, especially in the tracks.

Despite its shortcomings the Goliath was produced in substantial numbers, 2650 electric models and 5079 petrol, and it could be very effective when used in a favourable tactical situation.

Goliath Leichter Ladunstrager (Light Demolition Vehicle) SdKfz 303
Speed 12mph
Power plant Zundapp 12.5hp
Range 12km

Sdkfz 222

There were three basic family members that entered production in 1935-36; all based on the Horch 801 4x4 chassis. The SdKfz 221 had a crew of two and was fitted with an open-topped turret with a single machine-gun and a short-range radio. The SdKfz.222 differed from the 221 in having a larger turret with a 2cm auto cannon, a coaxial MG and a three-man crew. The SdKfz 223 was similar to the 221, but moved the turret slightly to the rear to accommodate a long-range radio and a third crewman. The same chassis and body were used to create the SdKfz 260 and 261 radio cars, which dispensed with all armament in favour of long-range radios and frame antennas. With thin armour (proof only against non-AP small arms fire) and weak armament, the initial members of the family were phased out of production, the last SdKfz 222 being in built in June 1943 and the last SdKfz 223 in January 1944. In spite of this the SdKfz 222 remained in service until the end of the war and served in all theatres of operations.

Weight 4.8 tonnes
Armour front and side 8mm
Length 4.80m
Width 1.95m
Height 2.00m
Engine HP 75 or 90
Maximum Speed 85km/h

SDKFZ 231 6 RAD; SDKFZ 231 8 RAD

The first of the new German armoured cars, these were built on 6x4 truck chassis strengthened to take the additional weight. The armament of the SdKfz 231 and 232 (6rad) was a 2cm KwK30 cannon and a coaxial MG 13 in the turret, with elevation of -12° to +20°. The SdKfz 263 had a fixed superstructure with a single MG13 instead of a turret. The SdKfz 232 had a large frame antenna, while the SdKfz 263 had the frame antenna and a telescoping mast antenna. The first two were used by reconnaissance troops and the SdKfz 263 by signal troops. The crew consisted of four, including front and rear drivers. Production ran from 1932-35, by which time about 1000 had been built. They fought throughout the campaigns in Poland, the Low Countries and France, but were withdrawn from frontline service in 1940 as the much-improved SdKfz 231 (8rad) series entered service.

Weight 5.35tonnes
Armour front 8mm, side 8mm
Armament
One 20mm KwK cannon with 180 rounds
One 7.92mm machine gun
Length 5.57m
Width 1.82m
Height 2.25m
Engine 65hp
Maximum Speed 70km/h

Sdkfz 234/2 Puma

The Puma was the outcome of a German army requirement for an armoured car capable of tackling a light reconnaissance tank at close range; this was a desirable asset since early contact with enemy attacks was most often at reconnaissance unit level. This vehicle retained the basic ARK series eight-wheel chassis but had a new heavier turret, with a 50mm KwK39/1 L/60 tank gun in a streamlined Saukopf (pig's head) mantlet. The turret had originally been developed for the abortive Leopard tank. The 50mm gun was very effective for its calibre, having semi-automatic action at a muzzle velocity of 2700 fps when firing armour-piercing ammunition. The compact mantlet incorporated a recoil mechanism mounted above the gun, a telescopic sight, and a co-axial MG42. Three smoke projectors were mounted as standard on each side of the turret.

The weight of the vehicle was of course increased by the addition of the turret, to 11.5 tons in combat order. The mantlet armour was up to 100 mm thick, but armour elsewhere was as for the other eight-wheelers of the ARK type. The turret had full 360° traverse and the vehicle was fitted with radiotelephones as standard but could also carry long range Fu12 radio equipment.

Heavy Armoured Car
Length 22.3f t (inc gun)
Width 7.64ft
Weight 25,880lb
Speed 53 mph
Range early model 500 miles, late model 620 miles
Armour
Turret 40mm max, 100mm on mantlet
Hull front 30mm, side 14mm, all other plates 10mm
Armament
One 50mm KwK39/1
One 7.92-mm MG 42

LIGHT TANK MK VIB AND C

Originally based on the Carden-Loyd tankette of the 1920s, the Vickers light tanks were developed in the 1930s. Successive improvements were introduced in a series of marks culminating in the MkVI. This was itself developed over three versions the MkVIA, B, and C. Of these the Vickers MkVIB was by far the most numerous and of a grand total of 1300 tanks in the British and Commonwealth armed forces in 1940 around 1000 were Vickers light tanks. Of these all but 162 were MkVIs. Mobile and fast across country, the Vickers was widely used in the 1930s for policing the British Empire and in the early years of World War II. However, World War II combat experience proved them to be virtually useless in the face of enemy tanks. Their thin armour was easily pierced and their machine-gun armament was utterly inadequate on the battlefield. Lack of equipment forced the British to use them in combat rather than for their intended reconnaissance role, and the consequences were disastrous. The majority were left behind in France with the evacuation of the BEF at Dunkirk. The remaining few saw out their days as Armoured Observation Posts in the Western Desert, their reconnaissance role being taken over by the armoured car regiments.

Crew 3
Weight 5.3tonnes (5.2tons)
Dimensions
length 4.01m (13ft 2in)
width 2.08m (6ft l0in)
height 2.26m (7ft 5in)
range 201km (125 miles)
armour 8-15mm (0.31-0.6in)
Armament
one 7.7mm Vickers machine gun with 2,500 rounds
one 12.7mm Vickers machine gun with 400 rounds
Power plant
Meadows ESTL six-cylinder petrol engine developing 88hp (66kW)
Performance
maximum road speed 56km/h (35mph)
fording 0.76m (2ft 6in)
vertical obstacle 0.6m (2ft)
trench 1.5m (5ft)

CRUISER TANK MK I; CRUISER TANK MK IIA

The A9 design was originally classed a Medium Tank when it was first designed by Vickers in 1934. But with the polarisation of Army thought into Cruiser and Infantry tank roles in the 30s, the A9 was redesignated the Cruiser Tank Mark I, of which a total of 125 were built. The Cruiser Mark I saw some action in France in 1940 and again during the early desert battles but in service it proved to be too slow and too lightly armoured. One of its best design features was its suspension, which was later adopted for the Valentine Infantry tank. The main armament of the Cruiser Mark I was the 2pdr but some tanks carried a 3.7-inch howitzer for close support work and in this form they were known as the Cruiser Tank Mark ICS.

Crew 6
Weight in action 13,042 kg (28,728lb)
Maximum road speed 40km/h (25 mph)
Maximum cross-country speed 24 km/h (15 mph)
Road range 241 km (150 miles)
Length 5.79m (19ft)
Width 2.5m (8 ft 2.5 ins)
Height 2.65m (8ft 8.5 ins)
Engine 150hp
Track width 357 mm (14 ins)
Wheel base 2.21m (7ft 3ins)
Armament
One 2pdr with 100 rounds or one 3.7inch howitzer
Three 0.303-inch MG with 3,000 rounds
Armour (overall) 14mm (0.55 ins)

CRUISER TANK MK III, IV AND IVA

The Cruiser Mark III was designed by the Nuffield organisation; it broke completely with previous designs and set the pattern that would be followed by all subsequent British cruiser tanks. With the adoption of the innovative new suspension system designed by American Walter J Christie a tank was able to have a far higher running speed and an improved cross-country performance with no great increase in engine output. However when it was combined with a more powerful engine it endowed the tank with a remarkable degree of mobility, a characteristic of all Britain's wartime cruisers. However its development was rushed, and early trials with the new A13 design soon revealed a less welcome trait common to early cruisers, that of poor reliability. The Cruiser Mark III was fitted with an American designed Liberty engine, and Nuffield's carried out production, but only 65 were produced. Some of these saw action in France in 1940 and in Libya but in service the type proved unreliable mechanically and was also too lightly armoured for its Cruiser role.

Crew 4
Weight in action 14,237 kg/31,360lb
Maximum road speed 48 kph/30 mph
Maximum cross-country speed 38 kph/24 mph
Road range 149 km/90 miles
Length 6,020 mm/237 inches
Width 2,540 mm/100 inches
Height 2,591 mm/102 inches
Engine horsepower 340
Track width 257 mm/1 0.125 inches
Wheelbase 2, 108 mm/83 inches
Armament
One 2pdr with 87 rounds
One 0.303-inch MG with 3,750 rounds
Armour (overall) 14mm/0.55 inch

CRUISER TANK MARK IV (A13 MARK II)

In early 1939 Nuffield's first cruiser, the Mark III, was followed on the production lines by the Cruiser Tank Mark IV, basically an up-armoured version of the Mk III. The most obvious differ≠ence between the two marks was the turret, which was much larger on the Mark IV due to the addition of extra spaced armour to the sides. The Cruiser Tank Mark IV became one of the most important British tanks dur≠ing the early war years and 655 were produced, but in action the Mark IV proved little more successful than the Mark III, mainly due to its general unre≠liability and the retention of the 2pdr gun which proved to be too light dur≠ing the 1940 battles in France and the early Western Desert campaigns. The one redeeming feature of the early Christie cruisers was their speed, especially across country, which often got them out of trouble.

The Mark IVA differed from the Mark IV by having a co-axial BESA machine-gun in place of the earlier 0.303-inch Vickers. There was also a Mark IV CS variant. After 1940 many Mark IV tanks were used in the train≠ing role.

Crew 4
Weight in action 15,000 kg/33,040lb
Maximum road speed 48 kph/30 mph
Maximum cross-country speed 22.5 kph/14 mph
Road range 149 km/90 miles
Length 6,020 mm/237 inches
Width 2,540 mm/100 inches
Height 2,591 mm/102 inches
Engine horsepower 340
Track width 257 mm/1 0.125 inches
Wheel base 2,108 mm/83 inches
Armament
One 2pdr with 87 rounds or one 3.7-inch howitzer
One 7.92 mm or 0.303-inch MG with 3,750 rounds
Armour (overall) 30mm/1.2 inch

INFANTRY TANK MK I MATILDA

The design of the Infantry Tank Mark I began in 1934 and the prototype was delivered in 1936. By 1940 139 had been built. The design was a very simple, rugged two-man vehicle with thick armour but the main armament was only a machine-gun. It was intended that the small Matilda would operate at the walking pace of the infantry it was intended to support, indeed it was so slow and had such limited range that mobile operations were out of the question. Its only saving grace was that its frontal armour was impervious to any German tanks of the time, but with only a machine-gun armament it could do no damage to them either. In France in 1940 it proved to be an unsatisfactory vehicle and many were left behind after Dunkirk. Those remaining after 1940 were used for training purposes only.

Crew 2
Weight in action 11,186 kg/24,640lb
Maximum road speed 12.8 kph/8 mph
Maximum cross-country speed 9 kph/5.6 mph
Road range 129 km/80 miles
Length 4,851 mm/191 inches
Width 2,286 mm/90 inches
Height 1,867 mm/73.5 inches
Engine horse power 70
Track width 292 mm/11.5 inches
Wheel base 1,930 mm/76 inches
Armament
one 0.5-inch Vickers MG
OR one 0.303-inch Vickers MG
Ammunition carried 4,000 rounds
Front armour 65 mm/2.56 inch
Side armour 60 mm/2.36 inch
Rear armour 50 mm/1.97 inch
Roof armour 12 mm/0.47 inch

INFANTRY TANK MK II MATILDA

The first Mark II Infantry Tank was delivered in 1938, its design was entirely new and owed nothing to that of the Mark I. It had its origins in 1936, but early production was slow and by 1940 only a few units in France had been issued with them. The Matilda II was the most powerful tank available to the British forces in 1939 and 1940 as it was a modern, well-armoured design but it lacked hitting power due to the 2pdr gun installed. It was also difficult to produce due to its complex design, but when production ended in 1943, 2,987 had been produced. The thick armour of the Matilda II was one of its most valuable assets, and in France and the early desert battles it was proof against all German anti-tank guns other than the infamous '88'. But the Matilda (the II was dropped after 1940 when the Matilda I was withdrawn) lacked speed and the small turret ring prevented anything heavier than the 2pdr being fitted. It was replaced in front line units in 1942 although the Matilda did remain in use in the Far East until 1945 with the Australian Army where it was more than a match for most Japanese armour. Some Matildas were also supplied to Russia. There were five models of gun tank and several variants based on the Matildas.

Infantry Tank Mark II.
First production type.

Infantry Tank Mark IIA.
The Mark II fitted with a 7.92 mm Besa MG.

Infantry Tank Mark IIA*.
AEC diesel engines replaced by Leyland engines. Known as Matilda III.

Matilda IIICS.
Fitted with 3-inch howitzer in place of 2pdr.
Matilda IV.

Infantry Tank Mark IIA**.
Improved Leyland engines.

Matilda V.
As Mark IV with gear improvements.

Baron.
This was a turretless Matilda hull fitted with a mine 'flail' for mine clearing. The Marks I and II retained the turret - the Mark III had auxiliary engines for turning the flails mounted on the sides.

Matilda Scorpion.
A Middle East mine clearing flail tank - used at El Alamein in 1942.

Matilda Frog.
An Australian flamethrower installed in place of the gun.

Matilda Dozer.
An Australian Matilda fitted with a bulldozer blade for obstacle clearing.

Matilda with Inglis Bridge or Trench Crossing Device.
Two 'pushed' bridges for crossing gaps or trenches.

Weight in action 26,950 kg/59,360 lb
Maximum road speed 24 kph/15 mph
Maximum cross-country speed 12.8 kph/8 mph
Road range 257 km/160 miles
Length 5,613 mm/221 inches
Width 2,591 mm/102 inches
Height 2,515 mm/99 inches
Engine Marks I-II, 2 x 87 hp (AEC)
Engine Marks III-V 2 x 95 hp (Leyland)
Track width 355 mm/14 inches
Wheel base 2,070 mm/81.5 inches
Armament
one 2 pdr (or 3-inch howitzer on CS) with 92 rounds
one 7.92 mm MG with 2,925 rounds
Front armour 78 mm/3 inch
Side armour 75 mm/2.95 inch
Rear armour 55 mm/2.16 inch
Turret armour 75 mm/2.95 inch

Infantry tank Mk III Valentine

The Valentine was originally a Vickers private venture based on the considerable fund of experience gained with the A9 and A10 Cruiser tanks, and used the same suspension and many other components. In 1939 it was thus possible to order the Valentine infantry tank almost 'off the drawing board' and as a result of the development carried out on the earlier, lighter tanks, the Valentine was a reliable and useful vehicle. The first Valentines entered service in 1940 and

for a while they were used as Cruiser tanks as a result of the prevalent tank shortage experienced until late 1941, and in the desert campaigns they proved to be good fighting vehicles, although they were hampered by the 2pdr armament and the vehicle's lack of speed. In time the 2pdr was replaced by a 6pdr gun and eventually by a 75mm gun. The Valentine was one of the most widely produced of all British tanks (by early 1944 when production ceased 8,275 had been built) but after 1943 its value as a fighting tank declined. The Canadians also opened a production line and built 1,420 vehicles nearly all of which were sent to Russia.

Crew 3
Weight in action 17,700 kg/39,000lb
Maximum road speed 24 kph/15 mph
Maximum cross-country speed 12.8 kph/8 mph
Road range 145 km/90 miles
Length 5,410 mm/213 inches
Height 2,273 mm/89.5 inches
Width 2,629 mm/103.5 inches
Engine horse power 131
Track width 355 mm/14 inches
Wheel base 2,210 mm/85 inches
Armament
One 2 pdr with 60 rounds
one 7.92 mm Besa MG (co-axial) with 3,150 rounds
one .303-inch Bren MG with 300 rounds
one 2-inch smoke discharger with 18 rounds
Front armour 60 mm/2.36 inch
Side armour 60 mm/2.36 inch
Turret front armour 65 mm/2.56 inch

CHURCHILL MK VII INFANTRY TANK

The origins of the Churchill lie in the earlier A20 design. This was not a success due to many inherent design faults and the project was handed over to Vauxhalls who carried out a major redesign to produce a new prototype known as the A22. This hurried redesign was carried out in a year and as a result the A22 design, soon ordered as the Infantry Tank Mark IV and christened 'Churchill', displayed a wide range of teething troubles resulting in general unreliability and numerous breakdowns. These faults were gradually eliminated but the result was that many of the early production tanks had to be returned to the factories or workshops for major reworking. The first Churchills were produced in mid-1941 at a time when there were very few British tanks available and as a result production was rapid and the numbers involved were large. Vauxhalls became the parent company to a whole host of shadow factories and concerns that produced the large number of components needed for the Churchill. Throughout its service life the basic design underwent a multitude of changes, both major and minor, the most important of which were changes were to the armament.

Weight in action 39,661kg/87,360lb
Maximum road speed 24.9 kph/15.5 mph
Maximum cross-country speed 12.8 kph/8 mph
Road range 145 km/90 miles
Length 7.442 m/293 inches
Width 2.743 m/108 inches
Height 3.251 m/128 inches
Engine horse power 350
Track width 355 mm/14 inches
Wheel base 3,810 mm/150 inches
Armament
One 6 pdr Mark 3 or 5 with 84 rounds
Two 7.92 mm MG with 6,975 rounds
One 2-in smoke projector with 30 rounds
One .303-inch Bren LMG with 600 rounds
Front armour 101 mm/3.98 inch
Side armour 76 mm/ 3 inch
Rear armour 50 mm/1.97 inch
Turret front armour 89 mm/3.5 inch

CHURCHILL ARK; CHURCHILL A.V.R.E. (VARIOUS ATTACHMENTS; FASCINE, LOG CARPET, SMALL BOX GIRDER BRIDGE ETC.)

The British Army produced its first bridging tank at the end of World War I and experimented throughout the inter-war period, with further variations. The first Armoured Ramp Carrier, the ARK Mk I, appeared in 1943. This was a converted Churchill tank with the turret removed and a blanking plate with an access hatch welded over the aperture. Longitudinal track ways were fitted along the top of the hull with long folding ramps at the rear end. The ARK could be driven into ditches or against obstacles and when the two folding ramps were lowered it could be used as a bridge for other vehicles. Variants included the ARK Mk II, which differed from the Mk I in having long ramps at both ends of the track ways; and the ARK Mk II (Italian Pattern), which was constructed locally in REME workshop in Italy. This version dispensed with the track ways all together, crossing vehicles being supported directly on the top run of the ARK's own tracks.

Crew 4
Weight 38,385kg (84.450Ib)
Length 7.442m (24ft 5in)
Width 2.43m (8ft)
Height 2. 13m (7ft)
Range 144km (90 miles)
Armour 16mm (0.6in)
Armament none
Power plant one Bedford twin-six petrol engine developing 350hp (261kW)
Maximum road speed 20km/h (12.5mph)
Maximum cross-country speed about 12.8km/h (8mph)
Fording 1.016m (3ft 4in)
Vertical obstacle 0.76m (2ft 6in)
Trench 3.048m (l0ft)

Churchill AVRE

The Churchill Assault Vehicle Royal Engineers (AVRE) was borne out of the failure of the 1942 Dieppe raid where engineers were prevented from clearing obstacles by enemy fire. The tank was developed to transport engineers to the required spot and give protection, as well as carrying a heavy demolition weapon, bridges and other equipment; special fittings were placed on the sides at the front for attaching various devices. With a stripped interior to give extra storage space and a mortar capable of firing a heavy demolition charge, they performed excellently during their first action, clearing the way for the Normandy landings on D-Day (6 June 1944). They remained in service with the British Army until the 1960s but the concept was so successful that AVREs are still used, the current model being the Centurion AVRE. Numerous devices were developed for use with the AVRE including:-

The fascine
The fascine was developed from a technique used in ancient times and was resurrected during World War II to allow tanks and other vehicles to cross ditches or streams, generally using bundles of brushwood to fill gaps. Sections of the pipe were included in the centre to permit water to flow through the fascine.

The Bobbin Carpet
The Bobbin Carpet used a steel reinforced hessian mat to cover wire obstacles or soft ground to allow troops and wheeled vehicles forward to assault the defences. The bobbins were carried well above the ground. When required the weighted free end of the carpet was dropped to the ground, the bobbin automatically unwinding itself as the tank rolled forward over the mat. This was first used during the 1942 Dieppe raid.

The Small Box Girder Bridge
Developed in 1943, this was an assault bridge, designed to be carried on the front of the AVRE. The near end was supported on special brackets on the nose of the tank the far end was supported by a winch cable that could be severed by a small charge from within the tank. This would cause the bridge to drop into place. The bridge could be used to span a 30ft gap or scale a 14 ft wall and would support a weight of 40tons.

Onion and Goat
Onion and Goat were both demolition charges fitted to frames that could be positioned against obstacles by the AVRE, which then backed away, the charges being detonated by remote control

Country of origin: UK
Crew: 6
Weight: 38,000kg (83,600lb)
Length 7.67m (25ft 2in)
Width 3.25m (10ft 8in)
Height 2.79m (9ft 2in)
Range 193km (120 miles)
Armour 16-102mm (0.64in)
Armament
One Petard 290mm spigot mortar
One 7.92mm Besa machine-gun
Power plant: one Bedford Twin-Six petrol engine developing 350hp (261kW)
Maximum road speed 24.9km/h (15.5mph)
Fording 1.016m (3ft 4in)
Vertical obstacle 0.76m (2ft 6in)
Trench 3.048m (10ft)

CRUISER TANK MK VI CRUSADER

Developed in 1939 by Nuffield as the A15, the Crusader first saw action in Egypt in 1941. They proved fast and highly mobile thanks largely to their Christie type suspension, but mechanical reliability soon proved to be a problem. Early vehicles were fitted with auxiliary machine gun turrets beside the driver, but these were deleted in the Crusader Mk II. The Crusader's high mobility proved to be a great asset in desert warfare. Losses, however, were heavy and the Crusader soon acquired a bad reputation for vulnerability. This was somewhat unfair since the Crusader compared favourably with it's main opponent, the PzKpfwIII AusfG. The problem lay rather with superior German tactics. Rommel repeatedly luring the fast moving British armoured formations into well prepared killing zones where dug-in and pre-sighted 50mm anti-tank guns and 88mms decimated the British tanks. The tanks were at a serious disadvantage in this situation as the 2-pounder of the Crusader, whilst offering adequate armour piercing performance, fired a high explosive round that was simply too feeble to deal with dug-in gun positions.

Crew 5
Weight 20,067kg (44, 147lb)
Dimensions
length 5.994m (19ft 8in)
width 2.64m (8ft 8in)
height 2.235m (7ft 41n)
Range 204km (127 miles)
Armour hull nose 33 mm, glacis 20 mm, driver's plate 40 mm, front 30 mm, sides 14+ 14 mm, decking 7 mm, belly 10 mm, tai128 mm; turret front 49 mm, sides 24 mm, top 12 mm, rear 30mm
Armament
one 2-pounder (40-mm) Mark IX or X L/50 gun with 110 rounds
two 7.92-mm Besa machine-guns with 4,500 rounds
Power plant
Nuffield Liberty Mark II V-12 liquid-cooled petrol, 340-hp

CRUISER TANK MK VIII CENTAUR

The tank that was to become the Cromwell was designed around the Meteor, a modified version of the Merlin aero engine. Since all Merlin production at the time was earmarked for aircraft use, it was decided to fit the A27 tanks with the old Liberty engine, with the intention of substituting the Meteor as and when it became available. The resultant combination was known as the A27L or Centaur of which 950 were built. Many were later to receive the intended power plant. Of the remainder many were used for training, 80 were fitted with 95mm howitzers for use as Royal Marine fire support tanks on D-Day and others were converted as armoured recovery vehicles and anti-aircraft tanks. The first Centaurs were produced in 1942 by Leyland Motors.

Weight 28,874kg (63,600lbs)
Crew five
Armament
One 95mm howitzer with 51 rounds
Two 7.92-mm Besa machine-guns with 4.950 rounds
Armour maximum 76mm (3in)
Engine one Liberty liquid-cooled petrol, 395hp
Maximum speed 27 mph (43 km/h)
Range 165 miles (265.5 km)
Trench crossing 7 feet 6 inches (2.29 m)
Vertical step 3 feet (91 cm)
Fording 4 feet (1.22 m)
Overall length 21 feet (6.4 m)
Width 10 feet (3.05 m)
Height 8 feet 2 inches (2.48 m)

CRUISER TANK MK VIII CROMWELL

The origins of the Cromwell lie in a 1941 specification for a replacement for the Crusader calling for improved reliability, heavier 75mm turret armour and 65mm hull protection, the new six-pounder (57mm) gun with wider 60-inch (152cm) turret ring, a weight of not more than 24 tons and a more powerful engine to give a speed of 24 mph (39km/h). A production order was lodged with Nuffield in June 1941 for 500 A24 tanks based on the Crusader design with an up-rated 410hp engine. Known as Cavaliers, they were not a success and only saw action as armoured recovery vehicles and artillery observation posts.

Leyland had begun an A27 project, also based on Crusader, which utilized the Rolls Royce Meteor derivative of the Merlin aero engine, a vast improvement on the Liberty. Although the first vehicles were completed with Liberty power units they were designed to accept the Meteor when it became available. The first production A27(L) appeared in June 1942, the Liberty-engined tank being known as the Centaur I. Like the Cavalier, it was only used for training as a battle tank, but those vehicles modified for specialized roles such as the 95mm howitzer armed Centaur IV close support tanks, did see action in North West Europe.

Weight 27.5 tons (28 tonnes)

Crew five

Armament

One 75mm Mark V or VA (L/36.5) gun with 64 rounds

Two 7.92-mm Besa machine-guns with 4.950 rounds

Armour hull

nose 57 mm

glacis 30 mm

driver's plate 63 mm, sides upper 32 mm, lower 25 mm + 14 mm. decking 20 mm, belly 8 mm, tail 32 mm ; turret front 76 mm, sides 63 mm, top 20 mm, rear 57 mm

Engine one Rolls Royce Meteor V-12 liquid-cooled petrol, 600hp

Speed 38 mph (61 km/h); with modified final drive 32 mph (51.5 km/h)

Range 173 miles (278 km)

Trench crossing 7 feet 6 inches (2.29 m)

Vertical step 3 feet (91 cm)

Fording 4 feet (1.22 m)

Overall length 21 feet (6.4 m)

CRUISER CHALLENGER; CRUISER COMET

The need for a battle tank to accommodate the 17pdr anti-tank gun was foreseen as early as 1941, but the tank for which it would have seemed ideal, the Cromwell, was too narrow to mount the size of turret ring necessary to take the extra recoil forces. To provide some form of vehicle to take the 17pdr, a design study was drawn up with an extended Cromwell chassis with an extra road wheel, a widened centre section, and a new and rather high turret. The Meteor engine was used and Cromwell components were used where possible. The parent company was the Birmingham Carriage and Wagon Co, and production was ordered in early 1943, but production was slow. Performance was poor due to the weight involved and some armour had actually to be removed in order to reduce the load; and in March 1944 it was realised that the Challenger had no provision for wading gear and could not therefore take part in the Normandy landings or campaign. By that time the Firefly, a Sherman armed with a 17pdr, was in widespread use so the Challenger was used in North-West Europe only in small numbers during 1944-1945 and only200 were produced.

Crew 5
Weight in action 33,051kg (72,800 lb) Maximum road speed 51.5km/h (32 mph)
Maximum cross-country speed 24 kph (15 mph)
Road range 193 km (120 miles)
Length 8.15m (26ft 8.75 ins) Width 2.9m (9ft 6.5 ins) Height 2.77m (9ft 1.25 ins) Engine 600hp
Track width 394 mm (15.5 ins)
Wheel base 2.46m (8ft 1.125 ins) Armament
One 17pdr with 42 rounds
One 0.30-inch Browning MG Armour (frontal) 101 mm (3.98 ins)

CENTAUR DOZER

As the momentum of the Allied advance through N W Europe and into Germany increased it was realised that while the existing armoured bulldozers could still, under certain circumstances, be of service, a dozer that could move under its own power at the speeds generally maintained by armoured fighting vehicles was required so that any obstruction could be immediately cleared and not have to remain until armoured bulldozers could be brought forward on transporters.

Surplus Centaur tanks were converted to this dozer role by removing the turret and installing a winch within the hull below the turret ring. The turret ring opening was plated over with hinged hatches provided for access to the winch. A dozer blade was carried on arms at the front of the Centaur and the winch was used to raise or lower the blade for obstacle clearance via block and tackle suspended on a jib fitted on the nose of the hull. The normal Commander's hatch in the top of the hull was removed and a raised box cupola was fitted over the opening to provide visibility for the Commander over the dozer blade. The only other operational uses of Centaur tanks were as AA tanks fitted with twin Polsten cannons, as turret-less armoured recovery

vehicles and as howitzer armed fire support tanks with the Royal Marines Armoured Support Group in the D-Day landings. The Centaur dozer first entered service on the 26th April 1945 and subsequently was of great service to the advancing armour by clearing lanes through rubble and other obstructions in many towns following the Rhine crossings. Centaur dozers remained in service with the British Army for some years after the Second World War.

A similar conversion was undertaken to produce the Centaur armoured recovery vehicle. Again the turret was removed and plated over and a winch fitted. This time however the winch was used for the recovery of stranded vehicles or in conjunction with a hull mounted A-frame to lift heavy components. Various piece of equipment such as block and tackles were carried on the hull.

Sherman Firefly; Sherman D.D.; Sherman A.R.V. I, A.R.V. II; Sherman Crab minesweeper; Sherman B.A.R.V.

The concept of using flails to clear mines originated with the Scorpion device first used on Matilda, Grant and Sherman tanks in the Middle East. It was further developed in the UK to produce the Crab, usually fitted to Sherman tanks. Some 43 chains were mounted on a revolving drum powered by the main tank engine. Further developments included the addition of barbed-wire cutting disks and, shortly before the end of the war in Europe, the Mk II introduced a ground contour-following device to ensure the detonation of mines left in depressions. The Crab retained the standard Sherman armament and it could be used in a combat role if the need arose. The drive for the rotor was taken by roller chain from the tank propeller shaft, through an aperture in the hull offside armour, to a Carden shaft. The drive from this shaft was taken by another Carden shaft to a spiral bevel double reduction gear on the offside end of the rotor.

Crew 5
Weight 31,818kg (70,000Ib)
Length 8.23m (27ft)
Width 3.5m (11 ft 6in)
Height 2.7m (9ft)
Range 62km (100 miles)
Armour 15-76mm (059-299in)
Armament one 75mm gun; one 7.62mm machine gun
Power plant one Ford GAA V-8 petrol engine developing 500bhp (373kW)
Maximum road speed 46km/h (28.75mph)
Fording 0.9m (3ft)
Vertical obstacle 0.6m (2ft)
Trench 2.26m (7ft 4in)

CENTAUR AA MK I AND II; CRUSADER AA MK I, II AND III

The original Crusader AA Mk I was a simple conversion that involved replacing the turret of the Crusader III with a Bofors 40mm anti-aircraft gun on a field mounting within a thin armoured shield. The more advanced AA Mk II model was fitted with a specially designed turret that offered much improved protection for the crew and mounted twin 20mm Oerlikon guns. The turret had a crew of two, a commander/gunner and a loader, while the driver sat in the hull front. The Crusader AA Mk III was almost identical to the AA Mk II model but the radio was moved from the turret to the hull front next to the driver to free turret space. The design appears to have been well thought-out, although the questionable mechanical reliability of the Crusader might have been a minor problem. By the time they entered service, however, the air threat had all but disappeared and they saw little operational use, for the most part being retained in storage in Britain.

Crew 3
Weight 19.8 tonnes (19.5tons)
Length 5.96m
Width 2.61m
Height 2.25m
Front Armour 51mm
Side Armour n/a
Engine 340 horsepower Nuffield Liberty petrol
Road Speed 45km/h (28 mph)

CRUSADER 17PDR GUN TRACTOR

The Crusader 17pdr Gun Tractor utilised the hulls of obsolete Crusader gun tanks to provide a highly mobile tractor for the potent but rather hefty 17pdr anti-tank gun. The conversion involved the removal of the tank's turret to be replaced with a lightly armoured open-topped superstructure. Various stowage lockers were also provided for ammunition and the various tools and pieces of equipment associated with the gun. The Gun Tractor entered service in 1944, serving in North West Europe until the cessation of hostilities. It was generally successful, offering greater cross-country mobility than wheeled tractors and good speed for a tracked vehicle, thanks to its Cruiser tank heritage. Reliability, which had been something of an issue with the gun tank was much improved since the Tractor was considerably lighter and the engine and drive train therefore much less stressed.

Crew 2 plus gun crew
Dimensions
length 5.994m (19ft 8in)
width 2.64m (8ft 8in)
Range 204km (127 miles)
≠Armour hull nose 33mm, glacis 20mm, driver's plate 40mm, front 30mm, sides 14+14mm, decking mm, belly 10mm, tail 28mm
Power plant
Nuffield Liberty Mark II V-12 liquid-cooled petrol, 340-hp
Performance
maximum road speed 434km/h (27mph)
maximum cross countryspeed 24km/h (15mph)
fording 1m (3ft 3in)
vertical obstacle 0.6m (2ft 3in)
trench 2.29 (7ft 6in)

SEXTON 25 PDR

The Sexton was designed in 1942 in response to a British General Staff requirement for a vehicle comparable to the M7 Priest in mobility and operational effectiveness, but mounting the British 25pdr field in place of the American 105mm howitzer. The vehicle selected to form the basis of the new design was the Canadian Ram , itself based on the American M3 medium tank. The Ram was, by 1942, obsolete as a battle tank and so the chassis were available for other applications. Layout was similar to the M7, but the driver's position was on the right, with the gun offset to the left since the Ram chassis on which it was based had the driver on the right. A small ammunition loading hatch was provided in the left side of the hull and the Sexton lacked the distinctive 'pulpit' for the AA machine gun that characterised the M7. The standard 25pdr was mounted but its recoil had to be restricted in order to prevent the breech striking the floor of the vehicle when fired at high elevations.

Crew 6
Power plant Continental R-975 air-cooled radial engine, producing 400hp. Maximum road speed 25mph and
Maximum cross-country speed was 20mph
Length 20ft 1in
Height 8ft
Width 9ft
Armament
One 25pdr howitzer MkII
Two .303cal Bren machine guns.

BISHOP 25 PDR

The Bishop was a hurried attempt to create a self-propelled weapon by mounting the proven 25pdr gun-howitzer on the chassis of the Valentine. The tank was too narrow to mount the gun within the width of the chassis, so a thinly armoured box-shaped superstructure was built on top of the hull. The vehicle carried a Bren gun on an open AA mount and 32 rounds of 25pdr ammunition. The improvised nature of the Bishop resulted in several shortcomings. In addition to the cramped accommodation for the four-man crew the vehicle had a high silhouette, making it harder to conceal. The gun was provided with a very limited traverse of only 4 degrees each side. More seriously the maximum elevation of the gun was only 15 degrees, which restricted its range to just over half that normally attainable (5,850m instead of 10,900m). The choice of the Valentine made sense in that it was one of the more reliable tanks available, but it also gave the vehicle a top speed of only 25 km/hr. They served in North Africa from the El Alamein battle, but were retired to training duties soon after, being replaced in British service initially by the M7 Priest and later the Sexton.

Weight 15.48 tonnes
Length 5.50m
Width 2.59m
Height 2.75m
Front Armour 60mm
Side Armour n/a
Engine Horsepower 131
Road Speed 25km/h

Archer 17 Pdr; Achilles 17 Pdr

The Archer was designed at a time when any method of mounting the potent 17pdr AT gun on an armoured vehicle was being considered in order to face the threat of the German Panthers and Tigers in the forthcoming Normandy campaign. The vehicle mounted the potent 17pdr anti-tank gun on the chassis of the proven Valentine tank. In order to accommodate this large weapon on a relatively small chassis the gun was mounted rearward over the engine deck in a fixed, low, open-topped fighting compartment. No machine-gun armament was fitted, although a Bren gun was carried for dismounted use and some vehicles were later equipped with an AA mount for a Bren or Browning .30cal machine gun. A total of 39 rounds of 17pdr ammunition were carried for the main gun.

Entering service in 1944, the Archer's slow speed, limited gun traverse (11° each side of centre) firing rearwards over the engine deck, and the fact that the driver's position had to be vacant in order to fire the gun limited its tactical usefulness. Nevertheless, the powerful armament and low silhouette made it a dangerous adversary and it proved a popular and useful weapon, remaining in service with the British Army into the 1950s.

Weight 14.4 tonnes
Front Armour 60mm
Side Armour n/a
Length 6.64m
Width 2.73m
Height 2.22m
Engine 192 horsepower
Road Speed 33km/h

FORD (CANADA) F15 WITH POLSTEIN AA MOUNT

The F15 was Ford Canada's contribution to 1.5 ton truck production for the war effort. Along with Chevrolet Canada, Ford accounted for the vast majority of Canadian production of 1.5ton trucks. The CMP (Canadian Military Pattern) trucks were all fitted with a range of standardised cabs, which were designed for ease of production and maximum interchangeability between the various sizes of trucks. The particular example shown is fitted with the Type 3 Cab, and is fitted with a platform body equipped to mount a Polstein 20mm AA gun. The gun was loaded onto the vehicle with a small hand winch up tubular ramps. The weapon's wheels were removed and carried on the sides of the platform.

Weight 6,272lbs
Engine Ford V8 producing 95hp
Wheel base 101.25ins
Length 173ins
Width 83ins
Height 86ins

DAIMLER DINGO SCOUT CAR

The Dingo resulted from a 1938 War Offfice specification calling for a small vehicle with frontal armour of at least 25mm, capable of resisting infantry light anti-tank weapons and able to head a column of tanks or other vehicles likely to encounter opposition. The vehicle was to be armed with a .303 Bren machine gun and should be able to withdraw quickly in reverse .For this reason only frontal armour was specified in order to save weight. Three companies submitted designs and these were tested in the latter half of 1938, with the one from BSA being selected. During the development of the vehicle the War Offic decided that the sides of the vehicle should also be armoured, the engine should be protected and that an armoured roof should be added. The vehicle eventually entered service as the Car Scout Daimler MkI, BSA having been bought out by Daimler. But was soon more commonly known as the Dingo, the name originally given to the losing Alvis prototype. The Mk Is all had four wheel steering but this was deleted in the Mk II as it caused difficulties for inexperienced drivers and at high speeds could cause the vehicle to roll over.

Crew 2
Power plant Daimler 18HP 6-cylinder engine, producing 55hp
Armour was to a maximum of 30mm
Weight was 3tons.
Armament
One .303 Bren machine gun
Length 10ft 5ins
Width 5ft 7.75ins
Height 4ft 11ins.

MORRIS LIGHT RECONNAISSANCE CAR

The Morris, and Humber, light reconnaissance cars were developed in 1940 to replace the earlier Beaverette reconnaissance cars that were produced as a quick solution to the shortage of armoured vehicles following the loss of BEF equipment at Dunkirk. The Morris had a 3-man crew, consisting of a driver in the centre, front of the vehicle and, slightly behind him, a gunner with a small open-topped turret with a Bren gun on his right and a radio operator to his left. The radio operator had a hatch that opened forward with a slit into which a Boys AT rifle could be mounted. The Mk I version had only two-wheel drive, but was replaced in production by the otherwise similar four-wheel drive Mk II. Although intended for use by the reconnaissance Corps, the Morris Light Reconnaissance Car was also used extensively by armoured car units of the Royal Air Force Regiment. In total around 2,290 of both marks were produced.

Crew 3
Weight 3.76 tonnes (3.7 tons)
Length 4.01m
Width 2.02m
Height 1.87m
Side Armour n/a
Front Armour 14mm
Armament
One Boys Anti-Tank rifle
One 7.92mm Bren machine-gun
Engine 71.8 horsepower Morris petrol
Road Speed 83km/h (51.5 mph)

HUMBER A/CAR MK I, II, III AND IV

The Humber Mk I was essentially the body of the Guy Mk IA armoured car fitted to the 4x4 Karrier KT4 artillery tractor chassis. This had the benefit of dramatically improving reliability, and the new engine also improved the power-to-weight ratio. Armament remained the same, one 15mm BESA and one co-axial 7.92mm BESA machine gun mounted in the turret. The Mk II featured a redesigned hull, with the driver's visor built into the front plate and a modified engine deck grille to clear the driver's line of sight when driving in reverse. The Mk III introduced a new turret providing space for three men, bringing the total crew to four. The Mk IV saw an increase in firepower, with the 15mm BESA being replaced by an American 37mm tank gun, though this necessitated the reduction of the turret crew to two men once more. Although overshadowed later in the war by the more technologically advanced Daimler, the Humber remained popular and was retained in service to the end of the conflict.

Crew 3
Weight 6.39 tonnes
Length 4.55m
Width 2.15m
Height 2.20m
Side Armour n/a
Front Armour 15mm
Armament
One 15mm BESA machine gun
One 7.92mm BESA machine gun
Engine 90 horsepower
Road Speed 75km/h

ARMOURED CARS, DAIMLER, MARK I AND MARK II

Introduced in 1941, the Daimler Mark I Armoured Car was first used in action in North Africa in 1942, and subsequently, in it's Mark II version, in Italy, North-West Europe and Burma. Many British and Commonwealth armoured car regiments used these cars and, after some initial difficulties, it turned out to be one of the best armoured-cars of World War II.

Inspired to a large extent by the design of the Dingo scout car, the Daimler Armoured Car was built to fulfil the armoured reconnaissance role of a light tank, and was therefore provided with armour and armament to a comparable standard.

The mechanical layout of the Daimler Armoured Car consisted of a rear-mounted, 95 bhp six cylinder engine from which the transmission was taken via a 'Fluid Flywheel' and pre-selector gearbox to a centrally mounted transfer box with a single differential. From this the power was transmitted via four parallel driving shafts and Tracta universal joints to each wheel, with final reduction gears in each hub.

Crew 3
Weight. 7500kg (16,500Ib)
Range. 330km (205 miles)
Armour. 14.5-30mm (0.6-1.2in)
Armament
One 2-pounder gun
One Besa 7.92mm coaxial machine gun
Powerplant one Daimler six-cylinder petrol engine developing 95hp (71kW)
Length 3.96m (13ft)
Width 2.44m (8ft)
Height 2.235m (7ft 4in)
Maximum speed 80.5km/h (50mph)
Fording 0.6m (2ft)
Vertical obstacle 0.533m (1ft 9in)
Trench 1.22m (4ft)

AEC ARMOURED CAR

The AEC Armoured Car was developed as a private venture by the Associated Equipment Company of Southall and provided some much needed firepower as the armoured car squadrons increasingly took on the light tank role of armoured reconnaissance. Based on the chassis of the AEC Matador 4x4 artillery tractor, the AEC was the heaviest of all the British armoured cars, and was provided with the heaviest armour. Normal drive was to the front wheels, with four wheel drive being engaged in rough terrain. The Mk I used turrets taken from early Valentine tanks that were converted to bridge layers, and were armed with a 2pdr gun and a coaxial 7.92mm BESA. The Mk II featured a slightly redesigned hull and a new turret with a 6pdr gun and BESA, while the Mk III replaced the 6pdr with a 75mm. The powerful engine and thick armour made it popular for specialized roles, especially in the heavy troops of armoured car regiments where they provided fire support for Daimlers and Humbers. It was a bit tall and the ground-loading a little high for general purpose usage, however.

Crew 4
Weight 12.9 tonnes (12.7 tons)
Length 5.40m
Width 2.68m
Height 2.67m
Front Armour 30mm
Side Armour n/a
Engine AEC diesel 158 horsepower
Road Speed 66 km/h (41mph)

ACV AEC 4x4 Mк I; ACV AEC 6x6 Mк I

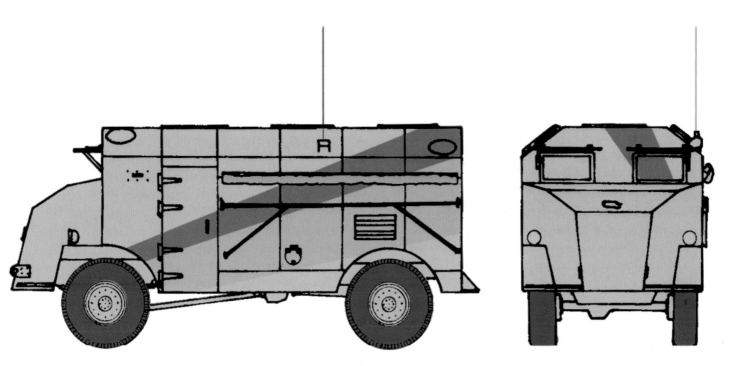

The AEC Armoured Car was developed as a private venture by the Associated Equipment Company of Southall and provided some much needed firepower as the armoured car squadrons increasingly took on the light tank role of armoured reconnaissance. Based on the chassis of the AEC Matador 4x4 artillery tractor, the AEC was the heaviest of all the British armoured cars, and was provided with the heaviest armour. Normal drive was to the front wheels, with four wheel drive being engaged in rough terrain. The Mk I used turrets taken from early Valentine tanks that were converted to bridge layers, and were armed with a 2pdr gun and a coaxial 7.92mm BESA. The Mk II featured a slightly redesigned hull and a new turret with a 6pdr gun and BESA, while the Mk III replaced the 6pdr with a 75mm. The powerful engine and thick armour made it popular for specialized roles, especially in the heavy troops of armoured car regiments where they provided fire support for Daimlers and Humbers. It was a bit tall and the ground-loading a little high for general purpose usage, however.

Crew 4
Weight 12.9 tonnes (12.7 tons)
Length 5.40m
Width 2.68m
Height 2.67m
Front Armour 30mm
Side Armour n/a
Engine AEC diesel 158 horsepower
Road Speed 66 km/h (41mph)

Ram Kangaroo

The Ram followed the automotive layout and lower hull design of the US M3 medium tank, but utilised a new upper hull and turret of Canadian origin. The first 50 vehicles were known as Ram Is and mounted a 2pdr and a coaxial Browning .30cal in the turret, together with a second MG in the small secondary turret on the left front of the hull, and a third on an AA mount. This was followed into production by the Ram II, which replaced the 2pdr with a 6pdr gun. Later vehicles eliminated the MG turret and side doors. It proved impossible to re-gun them with 75mm so they were obsolete by the time they entered large-scale service. They never saw combat as tanks, but were widely and successfully used as Ram Kangaroo armoured personnel carriers, with the turret removed and carrying up to 11 infantrymen. In this configuration the secondary MG turret proved useful. They were also converted for use as OP tanks, towing vehicles for 17pdrs, Badger flame-thrower tanks, armoured recovery vehicles and Wallaby ammunition carriers for Sexton SPGs.

Crew 2 plus up to 11 troops
Weight n/a
Length 5.76m
Width 2.76m
Height n/a
Front Armour 44mm
Side Armour 63mm
Engine 400 horsepower, Wright Continental R-975-CI or R-975-EC2 radial nine-cylinder air-cooled petrol
Road Speed 42km/h

TRUCK, 15CWT, 4x4. ARMOURED (GM C15TA)

The Canadian produced Armoured Personnel Carrier GM, also known as the Truck Armoured 15cwt 4x4 GM was a small APC (only 15ft 7ins long, 7ft 6ins wide and 7ft 5ins high) with a box-like hull, raised over the driving position, open topped and had a tarpaulin covered rear body. Designed as a replacement for the US White Scout Car M3A1, it had seats for eight passengers and was also used as a general load carrier. The chassis also served as the basis for an armoured ambulance, which had a slightly higher hull (8ft 11/2ins); and as a convoy escort vehicle, which was very similar to the A PC, but the rear of the hull was lower.

The Gm C15TA was in≠troduced in 1943 and proved extremely popular and successful in service. It was still in use with the army of South Vietnam in 1969.

Engine; GMC 270 6-cylinder, 269.5 cu in, 106 bhp.
Transmission; 4FIRX2.
Brakes; hydraulic (hydrovac).
Tyres; 10.50--16.
Wheelbase; 101 in.
Length 187ins
Width 92ins
Height 91in.
Weight 10,030lbs

BREN CARRIER

The original role envisaged for the Universal Carrier was for a fast, lightly armed vehicle to carry infantry across ground denied by small-arms fire and specifically, the Bren light machine gun and its team, hence the name Bren Gun Carrier. There was only one version of this vehicle named the "Bren Gun Carrier" but whatever the task, the entire family of vehicles was known by its users as Bren Carriers. In fact, numerous copies of the original Bren Carrier were produced and these were commonly known as the Universal Carrier.

The hull of these vehicles comprised a simple steel box with a motor compartment situated in the centre. In front, sat a driver and alongside him, a gunner. A radiator was mounted in a bulkhead between them, and the noise generated by the fan effectively drowned out any conversation between these crew-members as vehicles of this type were not fitted with any form of internal communications.

Crew 2-5 depending on the role of the vehicle
Power plant Ford V8 95/100hp water-cooled petrol engine
Length 12ft 4ins;
Width 6ft 9ins;
Height 5ft 3ins.
Armour 12mm max.
Armament usually consisted of one .303cal Bren Gun.
Maximum road speed 31mph
Range 159 miles.

NORTON BIG FOUR

Throughout the war the Norton Big Four outfit remained the only British military model to offer a sidecar wheel-drive, a feature widely used by European rough terrain machines. The Big Four was based on the well-established trials model of the late 1930s and incorporated several modifications to suit it for military service. The military pattern Norton was provided with a shaft running directly from the rear wheel and a simple dog clutch that was engaged by a left-hand lever when additional drive was required. The frame and rear forks were modified to accommodate the extra bearings. All three wheels were interchangeable and were fitted with 4in cross-country tyres for increased traction. A spare was carried on the rear of the sidecar.

Several thousand Big Four combinations were produced and it saw widespread use for reconnaissance and personal transportation in most theatres. The Big Four had always been slightly lacking in power for a cross-country machine and after several improved versions the War Office requested a replacement in 1942.

Power plant Norton single-cylinder L-C-A, 633cc, 14.5hp engine
Weight 679lb empty and 1232lb fully loaded
Maximum speed was 56mph
Length 7ft 2ins
Width 5ft 6.5ins
Height 3ft 10.5ins.

MORRIS COMMERCIAL CS8

The 15-cwt truck was one of the most widely used types in British service. Design of the 15-cwt WD-type infantry truck had been evolved in the early 30s and in 1934 Morris started series production. Two years later Guy Motors started producing their own design the 'Ant' and they were followed by Bedford, Commer and Ford with Canadian production of models from Ford, GM, Chrysler and Dodge coming online from 1940. The total number of 15-cwt trucks from all manufacturers in service in with British forces was over 230,000 when the war ended. The CS8, in common with most of the other makes, was fitted with several special body types including; water tank, office, fitted for wireless, wireless (house type), air compressor and tractor.

Weight 1.9 tons.
Power plant 6-cylinder petrol engine, producing 60hp.
Length 13ft 10.5ins
Width 6ft 6ins
Height 6ft 6ins

MORRIS COMMERCIAL CD/SW, BOFORS TRACTOR

The Morris Commercial CD/SW first entered service in 1937 and was a direct development of the model CD of 1932. It's appearance, however was vastly different as it was fitted with a light-weight, cut-away bonnet to meet War Office requirements and a completely new artillery body. The vehicle had no doors, weather protection being provided by canvas side screens. The cab and body both had soft-tops, and the overall height of the vehicle could be reduced to just 6ft 7ins with the tilts and windscreen folded. The original role of the CD/SW was that of tractor for the 18 or 25pdr field gun and limber and it was used extensively in this role by Australian and New Zealand artillery regiments as well as those of the British Army. With the introduction of the four-wheel drive Quad artillery tractors it was superseded in this role and was used instead as the tractor for the Bofors 40mm light AA gun. In this role the CD/SW carried 192 rounds of ammunition in external lockers, a spare wheel for the gun and a replacement gun barrel. The body also incorporated accommodation for the five man gun crew. The CD/SW was also produced as a light weight breakdown truck with a special body mounting a jib with a 1ton hoist and housing all the equipment necessary to it's role.

Crew 6
Power plant 6-cylinder petrol engine, producing 60hp
Length 17ft 2.5ins
Width 7ft 4ins
Height 7ft 6ins (6ft 7ins with tilts folded).

MORRIS COMMERCIAL C8/P, 17PDR TRACTOR

The history of the C8/AT goes back to the mid-30s when the War Office issued a request for manufacturers of 15cwt 4 x 2 infantry trucks to develop all-wheel-drive versions of these vehicles for use as artillery tractors. The first to be developed was Guy Motors' Quad-Ant, which entered production in 1938. This was closely followed by the Morris vehicle, the Field Artillery Tractor, 4 x 4, Morris C8. The C8 was a four-wheel drive derivative of the Morris Commercial CS8. The new vehicle was provided with a steel, fully enclosed body designed specifically for the field artillery tractor role and was a significant improvement over previous tractors. The C8 chassis was also used for other types of body including ; general service, a self-propelled Bofors 40mm AA gun platform, a predictor vehicle for use in conjunction with the self-propelled Bofors, and a 2pdr portee. It was these last two that, becoming obsolete due to advances in military technology, became surplus to requirements at about the time the new 17pdr towed anti-tank gun was entering service. The predictor and portee vehicles were rebuilt as tractors for the 17pdr. The conversion involved the fitting of a GS type body, providing accommodation for the seven-man gun crew plus the driver.

Crew 8
Loaded weight was 4.95tons.
Power plant 4-cylinder petrol engine, producing 70bhp
Length 14ft 3ins
Width 7ft 3ins
Height 9ft

MORRIS COMMERCIAL QUAD 25PDR TRACTOR

The history of the C8/AT goes back to the mid-30s when the War Office issued a request for manufacturers of 15cwt 4 x 2 infantry trucks to develop all-wheel-drive versions of these vehicles for use as artillery tractors. The first to be developed was Guy Motors' Quad-Ant, which entered production in 1938. This was closely followed by the Morris vehicle, the Field Artillery Tractor, 4 x 4, Morris C8. The C8 was a four-wheel drive derivative of the Morris Commercial CS8. The new vehicle was provided with a steel, fully enclosed body designed specifically for the field artillery tractor role and was a significant improvement over previous tractors. The Morris C8 artillery tractor was one of the most successful of the range of vehicles produced by Morris for the British Army. Popularly known as the Quad, the vehicle was introduced in 1939. It was used to tow the 18- or 25-pounder gun and was equipped with a 4,000kg (8,800 lb) winch. Inside there was room for the gun crew of . The Morris C8 was a sturdy vehicle with good cross-country mobility and adequate stowage space for ammunition. Early models had a distinctive beetle shape, but from 1944 onwards the vehicle was fitted with an open top.

Crew 1
Weight 3,402kg (7,484 lb)
Length 4.49m (14ft 8.75in)
Width 2.21m (7ft 3in)
Height 2.26m (7ft 5in)
Range. 480km (300 miles)
Powerplant. Morris four-cylinder 35-litre petrol engine developing 70hp (52.2kW)
Maximum road speed 80km/h (50mph)
Fording 0.4m (1ft 4in)

AUSTIN K2 AMBULANCE

The British motor industry of the thirties made three basic types of truck, the 4x2, mostly normal control and based on civilian designs, the 4x4, which were specialised forward control models, and the 6x4 made with both driver positions.

The most common 4x2s were the Austin K3, Bedford OY and Commer Q4. The Austin was based on the civilian machine with which the Birmingham company had returned to truck man≠ufacture in 1939, after many years of making only cars, light vans and taxicabs. It was a straightforward design with a 3.5-litre six-cylinder overhead-valve engine, a four-speed constant-mesh gearbox and hydraulic brakes. The military version had an open cab and twin 3.4 x17 rear tyres on the early models, later versions having a closed cab and single 10.50x16 tyres. A shorter-wheelbase version was the K30, a 30cwt truck, and this was also the basis for the K2 ambulance, possibly the most famous Austin product of World War Two. The K2 replaced older ambulances in service from 1940 onwards, eventually over 13,000 were built.

Power plant Austin, 6 cylinder, 3.46 litre engine, producing 60 horsepower
Wheelbase 11ft 2ins
Length 17ft 11ins
Width   7ft 1.5ins

AUSTIN K5 GENERAL SERVICE

Originally intended to replace the 3 ton 4 x 2 and 6 x 4 chassis in British service, this goal was not actually achieved until after the war. Nevertheless large numbers of 3 ton 4 x 4s were produced during the war, the majority by Bedford (a division of Vauxhall Motors), Ford and Austin. The Austin vehicle, the K5 was developed to fulfil a specification issued by the War Office in 1939. It entered production in 1941 and by the end of the war 12,280 had been produced, making it the second most numerous of the British four wheel drive trucks after the Bedford QL.

All K5s, apart from the early production K5 YN models, had removable cab tops to reduce their overall height for shipping. The K5 chassis was fitted with a variety of bodies including: the general service, anti-tank portee, cipher office, machinery, and wireless to name but a few. The AT portee was fitted with a half cab and carried a complete 6pdr anti-tank gun on a flatbed body. The gun could be fired from the truck or towed behind. This arrangement proved successful in the open terrain of the North Africa, where mobility was more important than concealment, but once the desert war ended there was little prospect of using the portee in it's intended role and most were rebuilt with GS bodies.

Weight 3.75 tons
Power plant 6-cylinder petrol engine, producing 85hp.
Length 19ft 8ins
Width 7ft 3ins
Height 9ft 11ins or 6ft 8ins with cab top and tilt removed.

Bedford QL , QLD, and QLB

Vauxhall' s interest in this type of vehicle went back to December 1938 when engineers working at Vauxhall (Bedford's parent company) suggested the feasibility of producing a four-wheel-drive Bedford. The advantages of an all-wheel-drive truck for military use were obvious and the War Office were asked for permission to proceed with a design. The War Office, although interested, felt the project should proceed, but only on a low-priority basis. Vauxhall were already engaged in the development of 4 x 2 trucks in the 15cwt, 30cwt and 3 ton categories and these were to be given priority. The outbreak of war provided new impetus, Vauxhalls were asked commence construction of some 4 x 4 prototypes as soon as possible. The detailed specification was approved by October 1939 and the first prototype was ready for trials on the 1st of February 1940. The trials were remarkably successful and the vehicle was ordered into production in February 1941 under the Bedford designation QL.

Power plant 6-cylinder Bedford engine producing 72hp
Payload 3tons
Length 19ft 8ins
Width 7ft 6ins
Height 9ft 10ins

BEDFORD MWD; BEDFORD OYD

Developed from a 1937 commercial model the first 50 Bedford 15cwts were ordered in August 1939. All were to be portees for carrying the 2pdr anti-tank gun. This was followed in September, on the outbreak of war, by a further order for 2,000 vehicles. Of these 480 were portees and the remainder were GS trucks. A few weeks later an order was placed for a further 11,000 and this was subsequently increased still further, the Bedford MW was eventually to make up a large proportion of the 250,000 vehicles built by Bedford during the war.

The basic GS truck was intended as a transport vehicle for the infantry platoon but came to be widely used by all arms. Early production MWs had open cabs, folding 'aero' type windshields and canvas side screens, with a folding hood for bad weather. From 1943 a more enclosed cab with side doors, a canvas top and Perspex side screens was fitted, providing much better weather protection. Several special purpose bodies were fitted including the portee, water tanker, fitted for wireless, wireless house type and tractor.

Weight 2.25 tons
Power plant 6-cylinder petrol engine, producing 72bhp
Length 14ft 4.5ins
Width 6ft 6.5ins
Height 7ft 6ins (5ft 3ins with tilt and windshield folded)

SAS Jeep

The British SAS Jeep was based on the Willys MB or Ford MBA and was modified for use as a raiding vehicle in the harsh conditions of the N African desert. In addition to racks for Jerry cans of water and fuel the vehicle was equipped with sand channels to extricate itself from soft going. Armed with twin Vickers air-cooled machine guns removed from obsolete aircraft the SAS Jeep was used for hit and run raids behind enemy lines, airfields and fuel dumps being favourite targets as a lot of damage could be inflicted with relatively light weapons. In order to operate in the desert heat the radiator bars of the Jeep were cut-away to improve airflow to the radiator and a condenser was fitted so that boiling water from the radiator was kept in circulation rather than being lost. The SAS Jeep was also fitted with a sun compass for navigation in the featureless desert wastes. It operated rather like a sun-dial in reverse in as much as that if the time was known the angle of the suns shadow could be used to show a bearing. This was a very useful device as it was unaffected by the magnetic effects of the steel Jeep body.

Weight 2,450lb
Power plant 4-cylinder Go Devil petrol engine, producing 54 hp
Maximum speed was 50mph.
Length 11ft
Width 5ft 2ins
Height 6ft with the hood erected, 4ft 6ins with the hood down and windscreen folded.

HUMBER UTILITY

The Humber Heavy Utility Car was the standard staff and command car of the British Army during World War II (the army was the only fully motorised force when war broke out in September 1939). It was also the only 4x4 British-built four-wheel drive utility car employed. Production of the 'Box' began in May 1941 and continued until1945. Widely used, the vehicle remained in service until the late 1950s, testimony to the quality of its design. Its fixed steel bodywork carried six seats and a folding map table. In the desert, the fixed cab was sometimes replaced by a canvas cover. The Humber was unspectacular in design, but more importantly it did the job required of it, and was found in all theatres. Transmission consisted of four forward and one reverse gears.

Crew. 1 plus 5 passengers
Weight. 2413kg (s308Ib)
Length 4.29m (14ft 1 in)
Width 1.88m (6ft 2in)
Height 1.96m (6ft Sin)
Range. 500km (311 miles)
Powerplant. one Humber six-cylinder 1-L-W-F 408-litre petrol engine producing 85 hp (63.4kW)
Maximum road speed 75km/h (46 8mph)
Fording 0.6m (1ft 11 in)

CHEVROLET C15 (CANADIAN)

Although trucks in this class had been pioneered by Marmon-Harrington, and were also produced by Dodge, International and GMC, by far the biggest producer was Chevrolet. During the war Chevrolet produced a total of about 160,000 one and one-half ton all wheel drive military trucks. All Chevrolet 1 1/2 ton trucks were fitted with enclosed cabs except the M6 bomb truck that was fitted with a soft-top cab and folding windscreen, and the airborne cargo truck that was modified to enable it to be dismantled for transport in C-37 aircraft. Only a few of these were modified from standard trucks in 1944.

The Chevrolet 1.5ton chassis was produced in two main series, the G-4100, produced from 1940-41, and the G-7100 from 1942-45. It was fitted with a variety of bodies including; cargo with and without winch, cargo long wheelbase, panel, telephone maintenance, telephone pole auger, crash rescue, dump with and without winch, and airfield lighting. Truck was also supplied as a chassis/cab for special bodies.

Weight 8 tons
Payload 1.5tons
Power plant 6 cylinder petrol engine, producing 93 horsepower
Maximum speed 48 mph
Length 19ft 3ins
Width 7ft 2ins
Height 8ft 8.5ins (7ft 3ins without tilt)

CARRO ARMATO L3/33 AND L3/35 TANKETTES

Based on the Carden Loyd machine gun carrier, the L3 series proved disappointing in combat. The crew of two was seated side-by-side with the driver on the right and the gunner on the left. In the earlier L 3/33 the armament was a single 6.5mm Fiat Model 14 aircraft machine gun, but in the more numerous L 3/35 it was upgraded slightly to a twin mounting of 8mm Breda 35 MGs. The mounting could traverse a total of 40° and elevate from -20° to +20°. A small number of L 3/33s in North Africa had their MG replaced by a 20mm AT rifle. Some of each model were also converted to flamethrower vehicles, and others were built as command vehicles with RF-1-CA radios. About 2,500 standard L3s were built and their good cross-country mobility made them reasonably successful against light opposition in Ethiopia. The thin armour, poor visibility, inadequate and poorly mounted armament and lack of radio left the L3 hopelessly outclassed when confronting enemy armour.

Weight 3.4 tons (3.4 tonnes)
Crew two
Armament
Two 8mm Breda35 machine guns
Armour hull nose and driver's plate 13.5 mm, glacis 8.5 mm, sides and tail 8.5 mm, decking 6 mm, belly 6-13.5 mm.
Engine FIA T -SPA CV 3 four-cylinder inline liquid-cooled petrol, 43-hp
Speed 26 mph (42 km/h)
Range 75 miles (120 km)
Trench crossing 4 feet 10 inches (1.45 m)
Vertical step 2 feet 4 inches (70 cm)
Fording 2 feet 4 inches (70 cm)
Overall length 10 feet 5 inches (3.17 m)
Width 4 feet (1.4 m)
Height 4 feet 3 inches (1.29 cm)

Carro Armato L6/40 light tank

The Fiat L6/40 arose from a 1930s design based on the British Carden-Loyd Mark VI tankette. Intended primarily for export, the first production models arrived in 1939 and a total of 283 were built. At the time of its introduction, the L6/40 was roughly equivalent to the German PzKpfw II, but was never really suitable for frontline service. However, it saw service with reconnaissance and cavalry units in Italy, North Africa and Russia. Variants included a flame-thrower version and a command tank, the latter having extra communications equipment and an open-topped turret. In addition, a number of L6/40s were converted into Semovente L40 self-propelled anti-tank guns. Although roughly comparable to other contemporary light tank designs, the L6/40 was hampered in operation by only having a two-man crew. It was also slightly underpowered and its suspension did not lend itself to high cross-country speeds.

Crew 2
Weight 6800kg (14,960Ib)
Dimensions
Length 3.75m (12ft 5in); width 1.92m (6ft 4in); height 2.03m (6ft Si
Range 200km (124miles)
Armour 6-40mm (0.23-1.57in)
Armament
One Breda Model35 20mm cannon with 296 rounds
One coaxial Breda Model38 8mm machine gun
Powerplant one SPA 1SD four-cylinder petrol engine developing 70hp (52kW)
Performance
Maximum road speed 42km/h (26mph);
Fording 0.8m (2ft Sin); Vertical obstacle 0.7m (2ft 4in);
Trench 1.7m (5ft 7in)

CARRO ARMATO M13/40 MED. TANK

The M13/40 was a development of the earlier M11/39. As early as 1938 the possibility of mounting a more powerful gun on the M11/39 was being explored, but it was 1940 before the first prototype appeared, an order for 1,900 production vehicles following shortly after.

The M13/40 was a significant improvement over its predecessor. The main armament was now mounted in a revolving turret and although the maximum thickness of the hull armour was not increased all round protection was improved. The crew was increased, by one, to four men but the layout of the vehicle meant that the commander still tended to be overworked.

The M13/40 retained the engine, transmission and suspension of the earlier vehicle and while the increase in weight caused only a marginal drop in performance on paper, in practice the new tank proved sluggish in operation.

By the standards of 1940 the M13/40 was an adequate tank and was generally considered to be almost as good as the German PzKpfw III. They were to see action in Greece and Yugoslavia as well as North Africa, where large numbers were captured by the British and used to equip the Sixth Royal Tank Regiment.

A new model appeared in 1941, the M14/41. This introduced a more powerful 125hp diesel engine and improved air and fuel filters for desert service. Both models continued in production side by side into 1942 and some M13/40s were reworked to the new standard. Further attempts to modernise the design resulted in the M15/42 that was fitted with a still more powerful 192bhp petrol engine and had a lengthened and widened hull to accommodate the larger power plant. Only 82 of the new model were completed however before all production of medium tanks was halted, in March 1943, in favour of Semovente assault guns.

Weight 13.5 tons (13.7 tonnes)
Crew four
Armament
One 47mm Model 37 (L/32) gun with 104 (later 87) rounds
Three 8mm Breda model 38 machine-guns with 3,048 rounds
Armour
Hull nose 30mm, glacis 25mm, driver's plate 30mm, sides 25mm, decking 14mm, belly 6mm, tail 25mm
Turret front 40mm, sides and rear 25mm, top 14mm
Engine one FIAT SPA 8T V8 liquid-cooled diesel producing 105hp
Speed 19 mph (30 km/h)
Range 125 miles (200 km)
Trench crossing 6 ft 11ins (2.1m)
Vertical step 2 ft 11.5ins (90cm)
Fording 3 ft 3 inches (1m)
Overall length 16 ft 1.5ins (4.91m)
Width 7 ft 4ins (2.23m)
Height 7 ft 10ins (2.37m)

M13/40 SERIES

The M13/40 was a development of the earlier M11/39. As early as 1938 the possibility of mounting a more powerful gun on the M11/39 was being explored, but it was 1940 before the first prototype appeared, an order for 1,900 production vehicles following shortly after.

The M13/40 was a significant improvement over its predecessor. The main armament was now mounted in a revolving turret and although the maximum thickness of the hull armour was not increased all round protection was improved. The crew was increased, by one, to four men but the layout of the vehicle meant that the commander still tended to be overworked.

The M13/40 retained the engine, transmission and suspension of the earlier vehicle and while the increase in weight caused only a marginal drop in performance on paper, in practice the new tank proved sluggish in operation.

By the standards of 1940 the M13/40 was an adequate tank and was generally considered to be almost as good as the German PzKpfw III.

Weight 13.5 tons (13.7 tonnes)
Crew four
Armament
One 47mm Model 37 (L/32) gun with 104 (later 87) rounds
Three 8mm Breda model 38 machine-guns with 3,048 rounds
Armour
Hull nose 30mm, glacis 25mm, driver's plate 30mm, sides 25mm, decking 14mm, belly 6mm, tail 25mm
Turret front 40mm, sides and rear 25mm, top 14mm
Engine one FIAT SPA 8T V8 liquid-cooled diesel producing 105hp
Speed 19 mph (30 km/h)
Range 125 miles (200 km)
Trench crossing 6 ft 11ins (2.1m)
Vertical step 2 ft 11.5ins (90cm)
Fording 3 ft 3 inches (1m)
Overall length 16 ft 1.5ins (4.91m)

Carro Armato M15/42 med. tank

CARRO ARMATO P26/40 HEAVY TANK

Although classed as a heavy tank in the Italian army the P40 was actually a medium tank by international standards. It was armed with a reasonably effective 75mm L/34 gun with 75 rounds and a coaxial 8mm Breda 38 machine gun. The hull featured a much better shape than the earlier M-series of tanks, making much more use of sloped plates; but the suspension was still the old paired-bogey design. The diesel engine used on the prototypes proved unreliable and was replaced on production models by a petrol version. One serious shortcoming of the tank was the continued Italian reliance on a two-man turret crew, a loader and a commander/gunner. The other two crewmen, the driver and the radio operator, sat in the hull front. The P40 was generally comparable to the US M4 Sherman, with a slightly better gun but almost certainly considerably less reliable and with an inefficient crew arrangement. Delays in production meant that no P40s were in service at the Italian surrender, and all of the 20 or so produced were seized by the German army.

Weight {tonnes) 26,0 Front Armour (mm) 60
Length (.m) 5,75 Side Armour (mm) 50
Width (fu) 2.75 Engine HP 420
Height \m) 2.50 Road Speed (km/h) 40

CARRO SEMOVENTE 75/18 SPG

The first of the Italian assault guns, this vehicle initially mated the chassis and automotive components of the M13 medium tank with a new, fixed superstructure mounting the 75mm L/18 howitzer. The main gun had a traverse of 18° left and 20° right, and an elevation range of -12° to +22°. Forty-four rounds were carried for the howitzer in a mixture of HE and AP. A machine gun was carried for dismounted use or on an open AA mount. Here again, the vehicle was undermanned, with a crew of 3: a commander/gunner, loader/radio operator, and driver. Later vehicles used the M14 and M15 chassis. A command version sacrificed the main gun in favour of observation equipment, a second radio, a twin 8mm (M 13) or a single 13.2mm (M 14/15) machine gun fitted to the right front hull for close defence. The Semovente 75/18 was the best Italian AFV to see widespread service in the war and was used to support the Italian armoured divisions in the Western Desert and Tunisia.

Weight 13 tons (13.2 tonnes)
Armament
One 75-mm Model 34 (LIX) gun howitzer with 44 rounds
Armour
Superstructure front 25 + 25 mm. mantlet 50 mm. sides und rear 25 mm. top 9 mm
Engine one FIAT-SPA 15T, 125hp
Speed 19 mph (30 km/h)
Range 125 miles (200 km)
Trench crossing 6 ft 11ins (2.1m)
Vertical step 2 ft 11.5ins (90cm)
Fording 3 ft 3 inches (1m)
Overall length 16 ft 1.5ins (4.91m)
Width 7 ft 4ins (2.23m)
Height 6 ft 1 in (1.85m)

CARRO SEMOVENTE 105/25 SPG

The first of the Italian assault guns, this vehicle initially mated the chassis and automotive components of the M13 medium tank with a new, fixed superstructure mounting the 75mm L/18 howitzer. The main gun had a traverse of 18° left and 20° right, and an elevation range of -12° to +22°. Forty-four rounds were carried for the howitzer in a mixture of HE and AP. A machine gun was carried for dismounted use or on an open AA mount. Here again, the vehicle was undermanned, with a crew of 3: a commander/gunner, loader/radio operator, and driver. Later vehicles used the M14 and M15 chassis. A command version sacrificed the main gun in favour of observation equipment, a second radio, a twin 8mm (M 13) or a single 13.2mm (M 14/15) machine gun fitted to the right front hull for close defence. The Semovente 75/18 was the best Italian AFV to see widespread service in the war and was used to support the Italian armoured divisions in the Western Desert and Tunisia. Delopment of the semovente diverged into two separate paths at this point.

Weight 13 tons (13.2 tonnes)
Armament
One 75-mm Model 34 (LIX) gun howitzer with 44 rounds
Armour
Superstructure front 25 + 25 mm. mantlet 50 mm. sides und rear 25 mm. top 9 mm
Engine one FIAT-SPA 15T, 125hp
Speed 19 mph (30 km/h)
Range 125 miles (200 km)
Trench crossing 6 ft 11ins (2.1m)
Vertical step 2 ft 11.5ins (90cm)
Fording 3 ft 3 inches (1m)
Overall length 16 ft 1.5ins (4.91m)
Width 7 ft 4ins (2.23m)
Height 6 ft 1 in (1.85m)

OM 36M LIGHT TRUCK

The first OM Autocarretta da Montagna, the Tipo 32 (type 32), was introduced in 1932 as a 4x4 light, multi-purpose truck, intended chiefly for use in mountainous regions. Produced by Officine Mecaniche SpA of Brescia to a design by Ir.Cappa, the OM 32 was powered by an air-cooled diesel engine that proved very reliable and would stand up to hard service in extreme temperatures. It had independent suspension front and rear, and four wheel steering. The gearbox was mounted amidships and drove the front and rear final drives directly. A captured example was taken to the WVEE (Weapon and Vehicle Experimental Establishment) at Farnborough in England for thorough testing and the cross-country performance was found to be extremely good. 1936 saw the introduction of three new models. The Tipo 36P and Tipo 36DM were troop carriers, the 36P provided seating for ten plus the driver and the 36DM seated seven plus the driver and was equipped with a pedestal mounted AA machine gun. The Tipo 36M was similar to the Tipo 32 but was fitted with pneumatic tyres. In 1937 the Tipo 37, a slightly modified Tipo 32 was introduced.

Power plant 1616cc diesel engine producing 21bhp.
Length 12ft 5.5ins
Width 4ft 3ins
Height 7ft

GUZZI TRIALCE

The Guzzi Trialce was a specialised military motor tricycle developed for the Italian Army from the Alce motorbike. It was used for general load carrying and as a heavy machine gun carrier. The example shown here has steel reinforced locating holes in the floor of the cargo body to receive the spiked feet of a machine gun tripod. The maximum load capacity was, surprisingly, up to one metric tonne.

The Guzzi Trialce was produced from 1940-43 and was widely used throughout the war.

Maximum speed of 80km/h (50mph)
Gearbox 4 speed
Transmission shaft drive
Weight 334.75kg (783lb)
Length 1.81m (9ft 3ins)
Width 1.24m (4ft 1in)
Height 1.04m (3ft 5ins)
Maximum load capacity 1 tonne (0.98 tons)

AUTOBLINDA AB40

The Autoblinda 41 was designed to meet the twin requirements of providing armoured car suitable for the cavalry regiments and also for policing Italy's African colonies. It was of bolted construction, and drive was to all four wheels; all vehicles carried radios. All three models had an 8mm machine gun facing out the rear of the crew compartment but they differed in their turret armament. The AB40 carried twin machine guns; the AB41, by far the most common version, was armed with a 20mm autocannon and a coaxial machine gun, and the AB43 mounted a 47/40 tank gun and a coaxial machine gun. Cross-country performance was good but the armour was thin, although generally on a par with German armoured cars. There were two drivers (one facing front, one rear), a hull machine gunner/radioman, and, in the turret, the commander/gunner/loader. The AB41 could be adapted to run on railway tracks and was used extensively in this role in anti-partisan operations in the Balkans. The AB41 was the most widely used of the Italian armoured cars and saw service in North Africa, Hungary, Italy and Russia.

Crew 4
Weight 7500kg (16,500Ib)
Length 5.20m (171t 15in)
Width 1.92m (6ft 4.5in)
Height 2.48m (7ft 11.5in)
Range 400km (248 miles)
Armour 6-40mm (0.23-1.57in)
Armament
One 20mm Breda cannon
Two 8mm machine guns
Powerplant one SAP Abm 1 six-cylinder water-cooled inline petrol engine developing 80hp (60kW)
Maximum road speed 78km/h (49mph)
Fording 0.7m (28in)
Vertical obstacle 0.3m (12in)
Trench 0.4m (1ft 4in)

CARRO PROTETTO AS37 (10-MAN APC)

The Carro Protetto AS37 was an amoured personnel carrier based on the AS37 light desert truck. It could carry ten men in addition to the driver . It mounted an 8mm machine gun at the rear on a pintle mount. The lightly armoured body was open-topped.

Weight 3.5tonnes
Wheel base 2.5m
Length 4.7m
Width 2.1m
Height 2.1m
Engine four cylinder petrol, producing 57hp

CAMIONETTA SPA 43 (SAHARIANA ANTE AERA SPA)

Derived from the Autoblinda 41 armoured car, and built for desert operations, the Camionetta SPA43 was a long, low vehicle with a boat shaped hull and was fitted with a variety of armaments. Most often 20mm cannons that could be used against both air and ground targets. Characteristic were the double rows of jerry cans carried either side of the hull that extended the range to 800km, double the range on internal fuel alone. The SPA 43 was used by mechanised cavalry units for long-distance patrols.

Engine 110hp Fiat
Range 800km
Length 5.2m
Width 1.8m
Height 1,49m

TYPE97, TE-KE TANKETTE

Type 97 tankette could be used for scouting or, with a tracked trailer, in the re-supply role. The original gasoline-powered Type 94 tankette weighed 3,550kg with armour up to l2mm thick and was armed with a single 6.5mm, and later 7.7 mm, machine gun. A door was fitted in the rear to facilitate egress for re-supply duties. A tendency to shed its tracks resulted in its replacement by the heavier diesel-powered Type 97, some of which were armed with the 37mm Type 94 gun in lieu of the machine gun. The engine was moved to the rear, which made access easier but reduced the vehicle's utility as a re-supply vehicle slightly. Neither vehicle was equipped with a radio, limiting its usefulness in the scouting role. It was often pressed into combat duties, especially later in the war, for which its thin armour and one-man turret made it largely ineffective. Several variants of the Type 97 tankette were built for special tasks.

Height 1.79m
Front Armour front 12mm, side 10mm
Weight 4.2 tons
Length 3.7m
Engine output 65hp
Width 1.90m
Road Speed 4km/h

SO-KI ROAD-RAIL TANKETTE

Armoured Rail Cars had been designed in the 1930s for use in the campaign in Manchuria. The Japanese Railway Engineers designed a series of cars, built originally by the firm of Sumida, beginning with the Type 90, or 2590 (the Japanese year in which the vehicle entered service (1930 in the West). This was a turretted vehicle, which, although not armed, had provision for the use of crew's weapons. It was easily convertible from rail to road use, the wheels having solid-tyred discs with removable flanged rims. The next model, the Type 91, was largely similar, but could be adapted from 144cm gauge to 152 cm as used in northern Manchuria. The Type 93 followed, and again was similar, but had a fixed armament (a light machine gun), and was heavier. Although the Sumida vehicles were very useful on road and rail, it was realised that a tracked variant would be needed for rougher terrain. The result was the Type 95, built in Tokyo by the Gas & Electric Company. Fully-tracked, the vehicle also had four flanged steel wheels mounted under the hull. These were raised and lowered by hydraulic jacks, and the rear pair of wheels provided drive whilst on rails.

Length 4.53m,
Height 2.45m,
Width 2.5m.
Armour front 8mm, side 6mm, rear 4mm, turret (except top) 6mm, turret top 4mm.
Max Speed 72kph (rail), 80kph (road).
Range 335km (rail), 123km (road).
Trench 1.5m.
The vehicle was powered by a 6 cylinder air-cooled petrol engine.

Type 95, Ha-Go light tank

The Type 95, known as the HA-GO, was developed in the early 1930s to meet the requirements of the Japanese Army at that time. When production ceased in 1943, over 1100 had been built. The major drawback of the vehicle was that the commander had to operate the gun in addition to his normal duties, which impeded combat effectiveness. While this was acceptable when faced with infantry in Manchuria, it proved disastrous when up against American armour in the later years of the war. Despite later upgunning, the tank's poor armour and lack of firepower ensured that it was wholly inadequate. The Type 95 also served as the basis for the Type 2 KA-MI amphibious tank, which was widely used in the early Pacific campaigns of World War II.

Crew 4
Weight 7400kg (16,280lb)
Dimensions
length 4.38m (14ft 4in);
width 2.057m (6ft gin);
height 2184m (7ft 2in)
Range 250km (156miles)
Armour 6-14mm (0.25-0-6in)
Armament
one 37mm gun
two 7.7mm machine guns
Power plant
Mitsubishi NVD 6120 six-cylinder air-cooled diesel engine developing 120hp (89kW)
Performance
maximum road speed 45km/h (28mph)
fording 10m (3ft 3in) vertical obstacle 0.812m (2ft Bin)
trench 20m (6ft 7in)

Type97, Chi Ha medium tank

Introduced in 1938, the Type 97 was a four-man tank with two crew in the hull and two more in the turret. The manually-rotated turret was offset to the right and was irregularly shaped, with the 57mm low ≠velocity Type 97 gun facing front and the machine gun about l70° off to the rear. A second machine gun was mounted in the hull front. The hull and turret were of riveted and bolted construction. Power was provided by a V-12 air-cooled diesel through a 4FlR transmission. The fighting compartment was lined with asbestos to reduce heat. The Type 97 was adequate in the infantry support role, its 57mm gun firing a useful HE round but was almost useless against other tanks. Its main weapon was of much too low a velocity, at 1,370fps only half that of the British 6pdr (57mm), to have much amour piercing capability. These shortcomings were forcibly demonstrated when the Chi-Ha faced Soviet armour in 1938.

Weight 14.3 tonnes
Armament
One Type 97 57mm gun
Two 7.7mm machine guns
Armour front 25mn,side 25mm
Length 5.55m
Width 2.33m
Height 2.23m
Power plant Mitsubishi V12 air-cooled diesel engine, producing 170hp
Road Speed 38km/h

TYPE 2, KA-MI AMPHIBIOUS TANK

Designed by Mitsubishi, the Type 2 Ka-Mi was the only Japanese armoured vehicle to go into series production during the war that was not based on a pre-war design, although it did borrow some components from the Type 95 light tank. The Type 2 had a full-width superstructure, extending out over the tracks, shaped to provide firm anchoring surfaces for the large floats. These were attached at the front and rear for swimming by quick release locking bolts, three at the front and four at the rear, that could be released from within the tank. The front float was divided in two longitudinally and was designed to fall aside in two halves, when jettisoned so as not to obstruct the tank. Should the tank need to be re-floated the pontoons could be re-attached in 15 minutes by the crew alone without any outside help using a collapsible auxiliary jib. The floats were designed to fit in a standard military 3ton truck for transportation. Propulsion in the water was by means of two propellers, while steering was accomplished by twin rudders on the back of the rear float, controlled from the tank commander's position. The tank mounted a 37mm Type 1 gun and a 7.7mm machine gun coaxially in the one-man turret, and a second machine-gun in the hull front. The crew of the Ka-Mi consisted of five men driver, bow gunner, gun layer, mechanic and commander.

Mizu Sensha 26021 Type 2 Ka-mi amphibious tank
Crew: 5
Weight: 12.5 tonnes (with floats) 9.5 tonnes (without floats)
Armour hull front 6-12 mm, sides and rear 8-14 mm, turret
12-14 mm
Armament:
One 37 mm Type 1 cannon with 132 rounds,
Two 7.7 mm Type 97 machine guns with 3500-4000
rounds of ammunition
Length 4.83m (7.42m with floats)
Width 2.8m
Height 2.34m
Maximum engine output: 84.6 kW (115 metric HP)
Top speed: 37 kph (land) 10 kph (water)
Range: 170 km (land)
140 km (water)
Trench 2m wide,
Vertical step 0.75 m

TYPE4, KA-TSU SUB-LAUNCHED LVT

In 1944 the Imperial Japanese Navy laid down the specif≠ication for a fully tracked, amphibious vehicle to carry up to
4 tons of cargo or up to 40 fully equipped infantrymen. The purpose of the new design was for the supply of cargo or troops to the island garrisons of Japan's sprawling Pacific 'sphere of influence'. Conventional amphibious vehicle designs were carried and launched from surface vessels which would transport these vehicles to their zone of operations. However, in 1944 transport≠ation by surface vessel in the Pacific was fast becoming a hazard≠ous occupation since US submarine activity was on the increase and the Japanese held islands were rapidly changing hands. It was thus desirable to transport this latest design to the operational area by a relatively safer method, namely submarine.

The 3rd Military Technical Laboratory of the Imperial Japanese Navy set themselves the task of designing this vehicle to be compl≠eted as soon as possible and utilising as much standard equipment in order to reduce the design and manufacturing time.

The completed design was, like most amphibious vehicles ≠boat shaped But unlike earlier Japanese amphibious tank designs there were no external, removable buoyancy tanks in short the new vehicle was simply a boat on tracks For this design the 3rd Mil≠itary Technical Laboratory utilised the running gear of the Type 2 amphibious tank Ka-Mi, but with four pairs of road wheels per side instead of just two. The hull itself was some 11 metres long and 3.3meters wide with a typical bow section and a flat transom stern. The crew position was forward the and above the drive sprocket and was protected by 10mm thick amour plated box provided with vision ports the driver's position was located on the right.

For steering the vehicle whilst afloat a secondary conning position was located on the upper deck behind the crew compartment. It too was fabricated from 10mm armour plate and contained within its three walls a steering wheel, a voice pipe to the lower driving position (for engine orders) and a simple seat for the helmsman.

The direction of the vehicle was controlled by a twin rudder installation operated by a continuous wire cable from the helm to the rudder quadrant via several blocks situated on the upper deck and back to the helm. This method was very

much the same as that used on the earlier Ka-Mi amphibious tank. The upper conning (or steer≠ing) position was designed to hinge to the rear when the vehicle was loaded onboard its parent submarine.

Also on the upper deck were located six loading hatches for the equal distribution of the 4ton cargo, two machine gun mountings for local defence (one on either side of the upper conning positi≠on each mounting a 13mm heavy machine gun) and sufficient bollards and cleats for harbour use. As for the accommodation of the proposed 40 fully equipped infantrymen no seats were provided so it must be construed that the carrying of troops was a purely secondary task and then only for short journeys.

Tb overcome the need for the vehicle to be totally watertight which would have made it very expensive and somewhat heavier it was decided that only the engine and its ancillary equipment be protected against water ingress. For this purpose a watertight cylinder was located on the vehicle's centreline between the front driver's position and the propeller shafts. The 6 cylinder, air cooled, 120hp diesel engine was mounted within this cylinder on a sliding chassis and provided with access ports along the cylinder's supper surfaces.

The fuel and oil tanks were located above the engine and access to these was via watertight circular hatches on the upper deck. For normal use the driveshafts for both sprocket gearbox and propellers were connected through access ports in the front and rear hat≠ches of the cylinder. Prior to being loaded onto its parent submar≠ine the drive shafts were disconnected from the engine and all access ports closed down and made watertight. Whilst submerged the vehicle was allowed to flood, this water being discharged on surfacing via a Kingston type valve located on the underside of the vehicle.

Although no references can be found regarding the prototype and its trials the vehicle must have been reasonably successful because an order for 70 units was placed with Mitsubishi Heavy Metal Industries in Tokyo from mid 1944. Only around 49 Ka-Tsus were completed by the end of the war in August 1945. Specs

SUMIDA M2953 ARMOURED CAR

Used extensively in China, the Sumida Type 2593 (or Type 93) 6x4 was designed so that it could be easily adapted to either road or rail use.

On the rails it used six, flanged steel wheels. To be prepared for road use, it was jacked up on four built-in jack/roller units (mounted front and back), then solid rubber tyres (carried on the sides of the hull) were fitted and the vehicle driven off the railway track, using the short lengths of rail which were also carried on the hull, on to the road. It was claimed that this operation took only ten minutes to perform. The 7.5 ton, Type 93 had a crew of six, mounted a single machine gun in the turret, but there were weapon slits in the sides and a small observation hatch towards the rear of the roof of its large body. Dimensions were: 21ft 6ins long, 6ft 4ins wide and 9ft 9ins high. It had armour up to 16mm thick and top speeds of 25mph on roads and 37mph on rails.

Weight 7.5tons
Armament
One 7.7mm machine gun
Armour 16mm
Max speed 25mph road, 37mph rail
Length 21ft 6ins
Width 6ft 4ins
Height 9ft 9ins

TYPE 4 HO-RO 150MM SPG

The Japanese produced few heavy armoured vehicles, partly because they were deemed unnecessary based on experiences In China and Manchuria, and partly because their industrial capacity was inadequate for the task. The Type 4 was a self≠propelled howitzer using the Type 97 medium tank as a base. The howitzer was the old 15cm Type 38, and was itself introduced in 1905 and was withdrawn from service in 1942 but continued to be used in the self-propelled version. The Type 4 was poorly armoured and had a slow rate of fire, mainly because of the breech mechanism employed. The gun had a traverse of 3° either side, and a range of elevation of -5° to +25°. The Japanese were unable to produce them in large numbers, and they were deployed in ones and twos, mainly for island defence. They were hopelessly outnumbered against American artillery in the Pacific battles In World War 2. The Ho-Ni series vehicles were very similar and were also based on the Type 97 Chi-Ha chassis. They differed mainly in their armament. The Ho-Ni MkI mounted a short 75mm anti-tank gun, the MkII a Short 105mm howitzer, and the MkIII a longer more powerful

Country of origin Japan
Crew 6
Weight 13,300kg (29,260Ib)
Length 5.537m (18ft 2in)
Width 2.286m (7ft 6in)
Height to top of shield 2.36m (7ft 9in)
Range 250km (156miles)
Armour 25mm (0.98in) max
Armament one Type 38 150mm howitzer with 28rounds
Power plant one V-12 diesel engine developing 170hp (1268kW)
Maximum road speed 38km/h (23.6mph)
Fording 1.0m (3ft 3in)
Vertical obstacle 0.812m (2ft 8in)
Trench 2.0m (6ft 7in)

Type 2598 So-Da

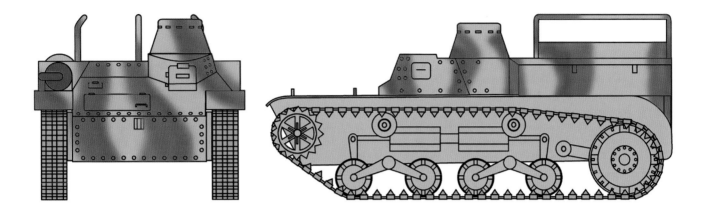

The Type 2598 So-Da was designed in 1937, based on the chassis of the Type 2597 Te-Ke tankette. It was used as both an armoured personnel carrier and a cargo carrier for front-line re-supply. Along with the serni-≠armoured body, it was fitted with a tow coupling so that it could also serve as an armoured artillery tractor or tow a trailer. The tow coupling was secured to the hull frame on a semi-≠elliptical spring. This arrangement protected the frame from distortion while hauling a heavy trailer, as well as safeguard≠ing the contents of the trailer from the results of sharp blows and jerking, which were common during cross-country travel. The So-Da hull differed in many respects from the basic Te-Ke, the engine was repositioned to the front, the hull was open≠-topped, and the flatbed had a large double door at the rear. Hull panniers, overhanging the tracks, doubled as holds for ammunition and other combat equipment. The flatbed could be covered with a tarpaulin, held up on three longi-tudinal rail supports. A six-cylinder air-cooled diesel engine gave the So-Da a top speed of 45 kph.

Crew: 2+4-6
Weight: 5 tonnes
Armour protection:
hull: front 6 mm, sides and rear: 12 mm
Armament: none
Length 3.86m
Width 1.93m
Height 157m
Maximum engine output: 47.9 kW (65 metric HP)
Top speed: 45 kph
Range: 200 km
Fording 0.8 m

TYPE 1 HO-HA HALF-TRACK APC

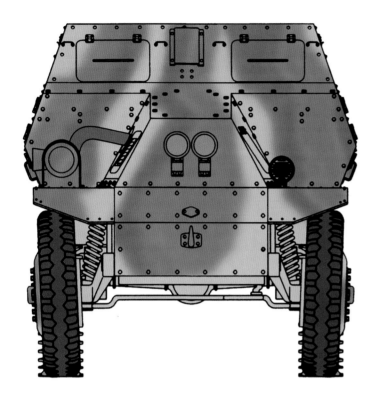

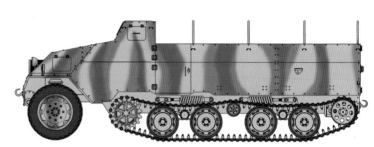

The Type 1 Ho-Ha was a half-track vehicle that served as an APC, cargo carrier and on occasion gun tractor, the long track length is suggestive of the German half-tracks, of which Japan received a few examples, and the armour was sloped in a similar fashion to the Sdkfz251 to increase its effectiveness. The vehicle carried a crew of 2 and 13 troops and was armed with three pintle-mounted 7.7mm machine guns. Access was by a door each side at the forward end of the troop compartment and a pair of doors at the rear. Passengers were seated facing inwards on benches that ran down the length of the rear compartment against the walls. In common with the German half-tracks, the Ho-Ha had an un-powered front axle, relying on the long tracked section for mobility.

Weight 7.0 tonnes
Armour front 8mm, side 6mm
Length 6.10m
Width 2.10m
Height 2.00m
Engine 134 hp
Road Speed 50km/h

TYPE 1, HO-HA HALFTRACK APC; TYPE 1, HO-KI FULL TRACK APC; TYPE98, SO-DA APC / AMMO CARRIER

The Type 1 Ho-Ki, was produced and used in three basic va≠riants: a basic armoured personnel carrier, an armoured supply carrier and an artillery prime mover. The engine was positioned at the front and drove through the transmission at the rear. The hull was of welded con≠struction, and open-topped. A hinged cover protected the driver's visor and there was a door in the left side of his compartment, behind that was the commander's sta≠tion with another side door. The driver's compartment was at the front beside the en≠gine, which was to the right of the armoured cab. The rest of the passengers (up to 12 men) used a rear door. The Ho-Ki could be armed, when needed, with one or two machine guns mounted in special flexible mounts on the sides of the troop / cargo compartment.

The Ho-Ki's six cylinder, air-cooled diesel engine was mounted in the front, to the right of the cab. Cooling louvers were installed in the front and side plates of the engine com≠partment, and the exhaust exited from the right side.

Crew: 2+12
Weight: 9 tonnes
Armour hull front 6 mm, sides 4 mm
Armament: none
Length: 4600-4800 mm
Width: 2100-2190 mm
Height: 2500-2580 mm
Maximum engine output: 66.2 kW (90 metric HP)
Maximum speed: 45 kph
Range: 200 km

BT7 FAST TANK

The original BT2 consisted of the Model1930 tank, designed by American engineer Walter J Christie fitted with a new, machine gun armed, one-man turret. The Christie designed suspension was well suited to the vast Russian landscape, as it enabled the tank to travel at much higher speeds than its contemporaries. For travel to the battlefront the tracks cold be removed, the vehicle travelling along roads on its road wheels at speeds in access of 50mph. The BT5 was similar, but was fitted with a two-man turret with the 45mm M32 gun and a coaxial DT machine gun. A more extensive redesign was undertaken to yield the main production variant, the BT7. Although still hampered by a two man turret, it had relatively heavy armour for the time, was fast and possessed a powerful armament. The BT7 acquitted itself well in the 1939 fighting against the Japanese, although there was little armoured opposition. By the time of the German assault in 1941, many were showing signs of wear and in any event they could do little to mitigate the effects of a lack of experienced senior officers, resulting from Stalinist purges.

Crew 3
Weight 13.8 tons
Maximum speed 46 mph
Road range 310 miles Cross-country 220 miles Length 18.65 f t
Width 7.98 ft
Height 7.50 f t
Engine M-17T Liberty, 12 Cyl petrol, 4&> HP Armament
One 45 mm L/46 A/TK gun with 172-188 roundsTwo 7.62 mm machine guns with 2394 rounds
Armour

28 MED. TANK

Inspired by earlier British and German multi-turreted tank designs, the T28 medium tank had a centrally mounted main turret with two auxiliary machine-gun turrets to the front. The vehicle's suspension was directly copied from the British Vickers vehicle, and though the prototype was armed with a 45mm main gun, production models were equipped with the more powerful 76.2mm low-velocity gun. There were a number of different models and variants, some of which were produced as a result of combat experience. The T28C, for example, was given additional armour on the hull front and turret as a result of the Red Army's debacle in the Russo-Finnish War. The T28V was a commander's tank fitted with a radio, which had a frame aerial round the turret and there was also a bridge layer variant that saw limited production.

Crew 6
Weight 28,509kg (62,720lb)
Dimensions
length 7.44m (24ft 4.8in)
width 2.81 m (9ft 2.75in)
height 2.82m (9ft 3in)
Range 220km (136.7 miles)
Armour 10-80mm (0.39-3.15in)
Armament
one 76.2mm gun
three 7.62mm machine guns
Power plant
M-17 V-12 petrol engine developing 500hp (373kW) Performance
maximum road speed 37km/h (23mph)
fording not known vertical obstacle 1.04m (3ft 5in)
trench 2.90m (9ft 6in)

T35 HEAVY TANK

The ultimate expression of the multi-turreted 'break-through' tank first inspired by the Vickers Independence of the 1920s, the massive T35 sported no less than five turrets. The main central turret was identical to that of the T28, as were the two MG turrets at the left front and right rear. The other two turrets each carried a 45mm Model 20Kgun and a co-axial MG. The tank required a crew of ten, including three in the main turret and two in each 45mm turret. Although enormous from the outside, inside the tank was cramped and inefficient. Unlike the T≠28s, it would seem that the T -35s were never re-armed with the longer L10 76mm gun. By 1939 it was clear their armour was too thin for a heavy tank, but the suspension was already overloaded so no improvement could be made there either. In the end it was their mechanical unreliability, however, that doomed them when they first saw combat in 1941, most being abandoned after breaking down.

Crew 10
Weight 46.1 tonnes
Armour front 30mm max, side 20mm max
Length 9.83m
Width 3.07m
Height 2.74m
Engine M17-M, 12 cylinder petrol, developing 500 hp
Road speed 37km/h
Road range 94 miles
Cross-country range 50 miles

T26 LIGHT INFANTRY TANK

This tank came in two main variants, the twin-turreted Model 1931, and the more orthodox Model 1933 with one larger turret. Each of the Model 1931's two side-by-side turrets, was equipped with a 7.62mm DT machine gun, although a command version substituted a 37mm gun in the left turret. The Model 1933's single turret was armed with a 45mm Model 1932 20K tank gun and a coaxial DT machine gun. The M1933 was by far the most numerous of the two and continued to be developed long after the M1931 had ceased production. It went through many changes, including the adoption of welding and the fitting of a second DT machine gun in the turret rear. The Model 1938 used the improved M1938 main gun. The speed was too slow for any but the infantry support role while the armour was too thin for that mission, and the two-man turret crew was inefficient. As a result the vehicle was not popular with its crews. Nevertheless, it had a good gun for its time and, on paper, was the equal of the PzKw IIIs sent into Russia in 1941. It was the most numerous tank in the Soviet Army in June 1941.

T26
Weight 9.4 tonnes
Armour front 15mm, sides 15mm
Length 4.62m
Width 2.44m
Height 2.24m
Engine 90hp
Road Speed 35km/h

Heavy Tank KV Series

The KV (later KVI) was developed from the twin turreted SMK prototypes that were tested under combat conditions in the Russo-Finish war. The SMK was unusual in layout, the main turret, armed with a 76.2mm gun, was located on a raised pedestal in the centre of the tank. The secondary turret was directly in front on the centre line but lower to allow the main gun a 360 degree traverse. Although generally successful the twin turreted design inevitably led to an inefficient crew layout. The large overall size also limited the thickness of armour that could be provided if weight was to be kept within limits. The design team leader Kotin pushed for permission to build a smaller, single turreted version of the SMK to be known as the KV for Klimenti Voroshilov Stalin's friend who was the Defence Commissar at the time. Subsequent tests and combat trials soon showed the KV to be superior and production commenced in 1940. The initial model KVI Ml939 featured the medium-velocity L11 76mm gun and two DT machine guns, one facing rear, in a three-man turret. In this case the commander doubled as the loader (the third crewman was a rear machine gunner), and it is unclear whether asking the commander to do loader duties was any better or worse than the T-34/76 arrangement of tasking him as the gunner. A third DT was placed in a ball mount in the hull front, where it was operated by the co-driver/ radio operator. The Model 1940 replaced the main gun with the longer F-32 and used the more powerful V-2K diesel starting in late 1940. In July 1941 production changed to the Model1941 , with the F-34 gun in a new cast turret with thicker armour. Applique armor was fitted to about a quarter of the tanks starting in the Spring of 1941 , to produce the KV-lE. A flame-thrower version of the KV-l was produced as the KV-8, in which an ATO-41 flame-thrower replaced the coaxial MG, and a 45mm M32 gun replaced the 76mm to create more internal space.

The KV-2 was a contemporary of the KV-l and shared the same hull and automotive components, but was fitted with a huge turret that mounted a shorted version of the l52mm M-l0 Model 1938/40 howitzer. The only ammunition available was the HE projectile with a reduced propellant charge. It was a single-purpose weapon, designed for the direct-fire destruction of pillboxes and other fortifications and was not built in large numbers.

The KV-1S was a redesigned KV-l with thinner armour, reducing the weight by 5 tons, and a new transmission, and consequently greater mobility. It also received a new turret with a commander's cupola and either the ZIS- 5 or F-34 76mm gun.

The KVI set the standard for Soviet tank design for several years to come and proved to be a formidable vehicle, being used as an assault tank to spearhead breakthroughs.

However, the tank was not particularly mobile and suffered from automotive

problems. In addition, it was up-armoured progressively without any corresponding increase in power, which resulted in poor power-to-weight ratio and performance inevitably suffered. In spite of these short-comings the introduction of the KVI proved a severe shock for opposing German forces. The standard German PaK36 3.7cm anti-tank gun was totally ineffective against the Russian tank's armour. Indeed there are several recorded instances of KVIs destroying anti-tank guns by the simple expedient of driving over them.

There were three main derivatives of the KVI

KVII

This was a close support version and replaced the original turret with a large boxy turret mounting a 152mm howitzer. The vehicle was a formidable opponent for the time, but the extra weight led to very poor reliability in a chassis that was already over-stressed.

KV85

The KV85 was the turret of the JS1 mounted on the chassis of the KVI. This was essentially a stop-gap type to get desperately needed 85mm guns into the field, pending the arrival of the JS1 itself.

SU152

This was the self-propelled gun version of the KV chassis and is covered elsewhere in this book.

KVI

Country of origin: USSR

Crew. 5

Weight: 43,000kg (94,600Ib)

Dimensions

Length 6.68m (21ft 11 in)

Width 3.32m (10ft 10.7in)

Height 2.71 m(8ft 10.7in)

Range 150km (93.2 miles)

Armour 100mm (3.94in)

Armament

one 76.2mm gun

four 7.62mm machine guns

Powerplant: one V-2K V-12 diesel engine developing 600hp (448kW)

maximum road speed 35km/h (21.75mph)

ording not known

vertical obstacle 1.20m (3ft 8in)

trench 2.59m (8ft 6in)

K V II HEAVY TANK

T34/76 MED. TANK

The T34 was an advanced tank for its era, produced in vast numbers to an excellent design, a design borne from two decades of Soviet experimentation and a readiness to embrace the best of foreign ideas. Mass production began in 1940 and its powerful gun and thick armour came as a shock to the German forces in 1941-42. Finesse was sacrificed for speed of production, but their rough and ready appearance belied their effectiveness. The T34 was used in every role from recovery vehicle to personnel carrier and reconnaissance, and distinguished itself at every turn forcing the Germans back on the defensive. It is no exaggeration to say that the T34 was the most decisive tank of World War II. The up-gunned T34/85 tank introduced in 1944 remained in use with many armies long after the war.

Crew: 4
Weight: 26,000kg (57,200Ib)
Dimensions
length 5.92m (19ft 5.1 in)
width 3.0m (9ft l0in)
height 244m (8ft)
Range: l86km (115 miles)
Armour: 18-60mm (0.71-236in)
Armament
one 76.2mm gun
two 7.62mm machine guns
Power plant
V-2-34 V-12 diesel engine developing 500hp (373kW)
Performance
maximum road speed 55km/h (34mph)
fording 1.37m (4ft 6in)
vertical obstacle 0.71m (2ft 4in)
trench 2.95m (9ft 8in)

T34/85 MED. TANK

The T-34 was developed by Mikhail Koshkin's design team at the Kharkov Locomotive Works as a replacement for the BT series. Incorporating features from several experimental vehicles including the A-20 and A-30 the new design provided an excellent balance between mobility, protection and firepower. The vehicle employed Christie type suspension, as had the BT series it replaced. The upper hull projected out either side to almost the full width of the tracks. This facilitated what was probably the most outstanding part of the design, the use of heavily sloped armour. This was a revolutionary idea at the time and like most good ideas is deceptively simple. The 45mm front glacis plate, for example, was sloped back at an angle of 60 degrees, but since an anti-tank shell travels on a horizontal trajectory it strikes the plate at an angle and must effectively penetrate 90mm of armour. So the protection offered by the armour is doubled with no increase in weight. The angle of the armour plate has another incidental benefit in that it tends to deflect shells rather than stopping them thus dissipating some of the shells kinetic energy.

Crew 5
Power plant V2 V-12 liquid-cooled diesel engine, producing 500hp.
Maximum road speed 34 mph
Weight 31.4 tons.
Armour
Nose, glacis, sides and tail 45-47mm, decking and belly 20mm
Mantlet 90mm, turret front, sides and rear 75mm, top 20mm
Armament
One 85mm ZIS-S-53 main gun
Two 7.62mm DT machne guns.
Length 26ft 8ins
Width 9ft 10ins
Height 8ft 6ins.

T37 LIGHT TANK; T38 LIGHT TANK

The T37 was designed as an amphibious scout tank with a two-man crew and was equipped with a turret mounting a single 7.62mm DT machine gun. This was developed into the T38, which was wider and lower than the T37, with better amphibious performance. Both models used the readily available power train and engine of the GAZ-M truck, simplifying maintenance and logistics. The T38 M2 switched to components from the GAZ M1 truck. A single propeller provided propulsion in the water at about 6 km/h and a rudder was mounted at the rear. A small number of T38s were modified in the field to replace the DT machine gun with a 20mm ShVAK autocannon. Only platoon and company commander vehicles were fitted with radios, a factor that limited the effectiveness of the non-fitted vehicles in their reconnaissance role. The very thin armour, necessary to maintain buoyancy, together with weak armament made them ineffectual in combat, and such vehicles as were still serviceable in 1941 were quickly destroyed.

Weight 3.2 tonnes
Armour front 9mm, side 6mm
Engine GAZ 40hp
Road Speed (km/h) 35km/h
Length 3.75m
Width 2.10m
Height 1.82m

T40 light tank; T60 light Inf tank

The T40 was the successor to the T38, with slightly thicker armour and a much better shaped hull. Armament was also improved, with a 12.7mm DshK heavy machine gun and a co-axial 7.62mm DT. Greater attention was also paid to waterborne characteristics and the T40 performed better there than its predecessors. However it was soon felt that too many compromises had to be made in fighting ability to make the tank amphibious. Starting in July 1941 work was started on a new design that abandoned these amphibious features. The chassis, suspension and power train of the T40 were used to create the non-amphibious T60 light tank. Armour was thicker and it was armed with a 20mm TNSh-1 gun with 180 rounds and a co-axial 7.62mm DT. Shortages of the normal CAl-202 engine led to other engines being installed as available, including Ford V-8s and CAl-M. Although built in fairly large numbers, the T60 had several significant shortcomings, including the two-man crew and, in most vehicles, the absence of a radio.

Height 1.74m
Armour front 33mm, side 25mm
Armament
One 20mm TNSh-1 gun with 180 rounds
One 7.62mm DT machine gun
Weight 6.4 tonnes
Length 4.10m
Engine CA1-202, 76hp
Width 2.30m
Road Speed 44 km/h

T70 LIGHT TANK

The Soviet military had spent a great deal of time and effort in the development of a series of light tanks during the 1930s. The T70 was the culmination of this effort at the time of the German invasion of Russia in June 1941. Reasonably armoured, the T70's armament was of limited use against heavier tanks, especially as the commander of the tank had also to load and fire the gun, thus reducing his combat effectiveness. Its service record was unremarkable, mainly being used for reconnaissance and close infantry support. Over 8000 were produced up to 1943, and it was reasonably successful in its reconnaissance role but at best only an adequate combat tank. It was superseded in production by the T80 with a two-man turret.

Crew: 2
Weight 9367kg (20,608Ib)
Dimensions
Length 4.29m (14ft 0.9in)
Width 2.32m (7ft 7.3in)
Height 2.04m (6ft 8.3in)
Range: 360km (223.7 miles)
Armour: 10-60mm (0.39-2.36in)
Armament
One 45mm gun
One 7.62mm machine gun
Power plant two GAZ-202 petrol engines delivering a total of 140hp (104kW)
Performance
Maximum road speed 45km/h (28mph)
Fording not known
Vertical obstacle 0.70m (2ft 3.6in)
Trench 3.12m (10ft 2.8in)

T50 Light Infantry Tank

The T50 was designed to replace the T26 infantry tank, but only a small number were built because of its high cost and complexity. It was nearly as costly to produce as the T34 and a good deal less effective. In fact by February 1943 only 63 had been produced and of these only 48 were armed. It served with a tank brigade in Karelia fighting the Finns where it was known as the Little Klim, a reference to its similarity in appearance to the KV tank.

Crew 4
Weight 14 tonnes
Armour Hull front 12-37mm
Armament
One 38mm Model 38 with 150 rounds
Length 5.2
Width 2.47m
Height 2.16m
Power plant V-4 diesel engine producing 300hp
Road Speed 60km/h

JS1 AND JS2 HEAVY TANK

Towards the end of 1943, and in anticipation of further advances in German tank design, a series of 21 tanks and self-propelled gun prototypes was produced of which six were accepted for mass-production. The most important of these was the JS1, or Joseph Stalin 1, heavy tank, designed by a team under the leadership of the engineer Kotin. The design of the JS1 tanks used clever armour distribution and an improved automotive layout to increase armour protection, whilst actually reducing the overall weight of the vehicle in comparison to the older KV series. Indeed although the JS was classed as a heavy tank in Russia it was almost the same weight as the German Panther medium tank. The initial model, the JS1, entered production at the end of 1943 and mounted the 85mm M1943 gun and complete turret of the KV85. This was almost immediately superceded in production by the JS2, equipped with a new turret mounting a 122m main gun.

Nevertheless, the front hull armour still proved vulnerable to large-calibre hits and in May- June 1944 production was switched to a design, the JS2m with a straight glacis plate rather than the stepped one previously used. The lower hull front, however, could not be altered. Armament consisted of the 122mm D-25T gun, along with a coaxial DT machine gun and a second DT in the turret rear. A DShK 12.7 mm MG was mounted on the commander's cupola starting in May 1944. The 122mm gun did impose two major drawbacks caused by the bulky, separately loaded, two-part ammunition. The rate of fire was only about 2 rounds per minute, and ammunition stowage was limited to just 28 rounds. On the other hand it did allow Soviet tank crews to engage enemy tanks at extremely long ranges and defeat any vehicle the German army could field at that time.

Crew 4   151
Weight 45tons
Armament
One 122mm M1943 with 28 rounds
Three 7.62mm machine guns with 2330 rounds
One 12.7mm DshK on AA mount
Armour bow 20mm, side 89-90mm, roof and floor 25mm, turret
30-102mm
Power plant V-2-IS (V2K) 12 cylinder diesel, producing 513hp
Max speed 23mph
Road range 150 miles
Cross-country range 130 miles
Length 22ft 4ins
Width   10ft 11ins
Height 8ft 11ins

JS3 heavy tank

During the final stages of the war, Kotin, the engineer responsible for the design of all Russian heavy tanks since the T35 personally observed the battles in which the JS2 tanks were engaged, and as the result was able to gain valuable operational experience. Subsequently, he produced the JS3 tank which entered service just in time to take part in the Victory Parade in Berlin during 1945. The basic alteration was to the distribution of armour. Thicker plates were used on the hull, sloped at greater angles, and the JS3 became the first tank to be fitted with a hemispherical shaped turret. This shape offers the maximum strength for the minimum weight and has been a feature of Soviet tank design ever since.

Crew 4
Weight 45.52tons (46,250kg)
Armament
One 122mm D-25 gun
Two   machine guns
Armour maximum 132mm
Engine V12 diesel producing 520hp
Road speed 23mph (37km/h)
Range 100miles (160km)
Length 22ft 4ins (6.81m)
Width   10ft 6ins (3.44m)
Height 8ft 11ins (2.93m)

PT34 (T34 fitted with Mugalev mineroller); T34 A.R.V

Mineroller tanks, designated PT-34, were developed by A. P. Mugalev in 1942. The PT-34 was a fairly conventional design with four thick banks of cast disks pushed in front of both tracks and was most often based on the T-34/76 Model 1943 or T-34/85 Model 1944.

The mineroller was attached to the lower hull plate with a large Y girder fork whiched allowed the assembly of roller disks to turn somewhat, however, when not in usem the roller assembly was removed.

The first experimental use of PT-34 tanks were on the Voronezh Front in 1943 by the 233rd Tank Bttn in the 86th Tank Brigade of the 4th Guards Independent Tank Regiment, as they had at least two experimental units of mine rollers in action. The first complete action of minerolling tanks took place in October 1943 with the 166th Independent Engineer Regiment attached to the 3rd Guards Tank Army. These regiments had 18 mine-rollers and 22 T-34 tanks.

SU122 AND SU85

The SU-122 was the first self-propelled gun to be based on the chassis of the T-34. It was designed in the summer of 1942 and ordered into production in December of the same year. The turret was replaced with a fixed superstructure, mounting the 122mm M30S howitzer. The SU122 was intended to operate as an assault gun in the direct support of tanks or infantry against defended positions, and could also be used against tanks; although the performance of the gun's HESH round was at best mediocre.
The gun could elevate from -3° to +26° and traverse 10° each side of centre. The crew of five consisted of a driver and gunner on the left, commander at the right front, and two loaders at the rear to handle the separately loaded ammunition. Forty rounds were carried for the howitzer. The first SU122 was produced at the end of 1943 and went into action the following January.

In August 1943 the SU122 was replaced in production by the SU85. The hull of the SU85 was largely unchanged from that of the SU122, although a new ball mounting for the main gun was developed that offered increased traverse and improved protection. This mounting was used on the last batches of SU122s before production was switched to the SU85. The new vehicle substituted the 85mm D-5S gun for the howitzer, and was the first Russian vehicle designed specifically as a tank hunter. One of the loaders was dispensed with at the same time since the rounds for the 85mm were less bulky. The first SU85s entered service in August 1943, and proved reasonably successful although with no defensive machine gun care had to be taken not to leave the vehicle open to attack from tank stalker teams. Production continued until the summer of 1944 when the arrival of the T34/85, which mounted the same gun in a revolving turret, rendered the SU85 redundant. The SU≠85M was the final model and mounted existing stocks of the D-5S 85mm gun in the hull of the SU100 pending the availability of the 100mm weapon. Specs

SU122
Crew 5
Height 2.32m
Armour front 45mm, side 45mm, rear 45, roof 20mm, bottom 20mm
Armament
One M-30S 122mm howitzer with 40 rounds
Weight 30.9 tonnes
Length 6.95m
Width 3.00
Power plant V-2 diesel engine, producing 500hp
Road Speed 55km/h

SU85
Crew 4
Height 2.45m
Armour front 45mm, side 45mm, rear 45, roof 20mm, bottom 20mm
Armament
One D-5S 85mm gun with 48 rounds
Weight 29.2 tonnes
Length 8.m
Width 3.00m
Power plant V-2 diesel engine, producing 500hp
Road Speed 55km/h

SU 85

SU 100

The SU100 was developed as a dedicated tank destroyer and mounted the 100mm D10S gun on the chassis of the T34 tank. The gun was mounted in a fixed superstructure that was similar, but not identical, to that of the SU85 and SU122 that preceded it. The fighting compartment was slightly roomier to accommodate the larger gun and the tank commander's position was moved towards the outside, with a pulpit-style cupola projecting from the side of the vehicle. The vehicle accommodated a crew of four and carried 34 rounds of ammunition. It had no secondary machine gun armament. The SU100 was quite nose ≠heavy due to the large gun and the limited ammunition stowage could be a tactical disadvantage. However, it was a very efficient tank killer, with a powerful gun and good armour protection.

Crew 4
Weight 31.6 tonnes
Armour Hull front 45mm, side 45mm, rear 20mm, roof 20mm, bottom 20mm
Armament
One 100mm D20S gun with 34 rounds
Length 9.45m
Width 3.00m
Height 2.25m
Power plant V-2 diesel engine producing 500hp
Road Speed 48km/h

SU152, JSU122 and JSU152

The SU152 was designed as counter to the German Tiger in a record 25 days. It was based on the chassis of the KV≠IS heavy tank, and a fixed armoured superstructure was built onto the hull in place of the turret to house the 152mm ML≠20 gun/howitzer. The vehicle was equipped with both a panoramic sight for indirect fire and a telescopic sight for direct fire, although the latter was the more common usage. The gun could traverse 12° and could elevate from-5° to + 18°. Ammunition was separate-loading, which limited the practical rate of fire to about two rounds per minute, and 20 rounds were carried. Both AP and HE rounds were available. No secondary armament was initially fitted, but a 12.7mm DShK machine gun on an AA mount was added during the production run. The SU≠152, with its massive HE shell, was a fearsome infantry support vehicle. It could also be used as a tank destroyer, although the curved trajectory of the projectiles made accuracy less than optimal for that role.

The first twelve production vehicles were rushed into action at the start of the battle of Kursk with a further nine arriving during the course of the battle. The SU152 proved to be one of the few Soviet vehicles that could take on the German Tigers, Panthers and Elefants, earning for itself the knickname of Zvierboy or Animal Hunter.

With the ending of production of the KV chassis in 1943, plans were put in hand to develop an replacement for the SU152 based on the running gear of the KV's successor the JS1.The prototype vehicle mounted the 152mm ML-20 gun/howitzer and was accepted for production as the JSU152 at the end of 1943 .The JSU152, was essentially an update of the SU152 concept and was very similar to the earlier vehicle. The fighting compartment was slightly taller than on the SU152. The armour was thicker but the ammunition load the same. Traverse was l0° each side and the maximum elevation gained an extra 2° due to higher trunnion mountings.

The JSU122, developed at the same time substituted l22mm A-19 gun as the main armament. This was essentially interchangeable with the 152mm ML-20 gun/howitzer since both weapons shared the same carriage and recuperator assembly. Extrenally both vehicles were identical apart from the gun tubes. The final production batch of the JSU122 mounted a modified A-19 was with a semi-automatic breech block and re-designated the D-25S

SU152
Crew 5
Weight 45.5tonnes
Armour front 60mm, sides 60mm, rear 60mm, roof 30mm, bottom 30mm
Armament
One 152mm ML20Sgun with 20 rounds
Length 8.95m
Width 3.25m
Height 2.45m
Power plant V-2 diesel engine producing 600hp
Road Speed
43km/h

JSU122
Crew 5
Weight 45.5 tonnes
Armour front 90mm, side 90mm, rear 60mm, roof 30mm, bottom 30mm
Armament
One l22mm A-19 gun
Height 2.48m
Length 9.85m
Width 3.07m
Power plant V-2 diesel engine, producing 600
Road Speed 37km/h

When this was fitted in lieu of the A-19 the rate of fire increased from 1.5 to 3 rounds per minute and the vehicle was designated the JSU122S. The new vehicle was also fitted with a ball type mantlet and a muzzle brake. The JSU152 carried 20 rounds and the JSU122 30 rounds of ammunition. Both had provision for a 12.7 mm DShK AA machine gun, and both were employed very effectively as infantry support vehicles, although the higher velocity gun of the JSU122 made it an excellent long-range tank killer as well.

JSU152
Crew 5
Weight 45.5 tonnes
Armour front 90mm, side 90mm, rear 60mm, roof 30mm, bottom 30mm
Armament
One 152mm ML-20 gun/howitzer
Height 2.48m
Length 9.18m
Width 3.07m
Power plant V-2 diesel engine, producing 600
Road Speed 37km/h

BA6, BA10 SERIES AND BA64

BA6 series armoured cars

Work on heavy armoured cars to replace the BA-27 started in 1932 at the Izhorskiy Factory. The first type was called the BAl and was based on imported Ford-Timken lorry chassis. A small experimental series was built, but it was not particularly well armed. Before production in quantity began, the new GAZ-AAA lorry chassis became available and this formed the basis for the new BA3 armoured car, which used the turret from the T26 Model 1933 light tank. Production began in 1934, but was short-lived because initial service use showed that the chassis was grossly overloaded. An improved version, the BA6 was designed using a strengthened rear suspension, a new transmission and a lighter armoured body. The BA3 and BA6 are very difficult to tell apart, though it would seem that one of the few apparent differences was the omission of a right rear access door on the BA6. At least three variants of the BA-6 were built. The BA6ZhD was a rail scout version with steel railway wheels substituted for the usual tyres. The BA6M was a modernized version produced in small numbers with a new lighter conical turret. The BA9 was a derivative of the BA-6M, armed with a 12.7mm DShK heavy machine-

gun in place of the usual 45mm gun. The BA6M was thoroughly re-designed in 1938, to produce the BA10. This used the conical turret of the BA6M, but the body design was lightened and improved. It was produced at the Izhorskiy Factory until the outbreak of the war and was the standard heavy armoured car of the RKKA even throughout the Great Patriotic War. A rail scout version, the BA≠10ZhD was built in small numbers. In 1939, the design bureau at the Izhorskiy Factory tried to develop a BAl0 derivative on the ZiS-6 lorry chassis which had greater horse≠power. A small series was built in 1940 in both a petrol engine version, the BA11, and in a further modernized type with diesel engine, the BA11D. However, this type did not supersede the BA-l0.

BA6
Crew 4
Weight 5.1 tonnes
Length 4.65m
Width 2.1m
Height 2.2m
Armour 10mm

Armament
One 45mm gun
Power plant GAZ-A petrol engine, producing 40 hp
Maximum speed 55km/h

BA10
Crew 4
Weight 5.1 tonnes
Length 4.65m
Width 2.1m
Height 2.2m
Armour 6-15mm
Armament
One 45mm gun
Power plant GAZ-M1 petrol engine, producing 50 hp
Maximum speed 55km/h

BA64 armoured car
The BA64 was the only new armoured car to be introduced by the Soviet Union during the war there being large stocks of the BA10 heavy armoured car available even as late as 1943. The BA-64 was a small, two-man 2.36ton scout car, powered by a 50hp four-cylinder GAZ-MM engine. Based on the GAZ-64 type jeep and designed mainly for liaison work, the two-man BA-64A car was also extensively used for transporting officers, reconnaissance and other tasks. It was designed and produced by GAZ, but shows distinct German influences in its body shape and armour design. Dimensions were 12ft long, 5ft wide and 6ft 3ins high, the car had a top speed of 50mph and a range of 280 miles. When the GAZ-67b type jeep entered service, the BA-64b

became the production model, the main difference being that the 7.62mm machine gun was now mounted in a small turret rather than being pintle-mounted at the front of the open top. This well-liked diminutive vehicle was affectionately known as Bobik by its crews. Total wartime production was about 3,500.

Variants included:
BA64 with DShK 1938 MG. Was a model that mounted a 12.7mm heavy machine-gun on top of the scout car's existing open-topped turret. It was built in small numbers during 1944.
BASh64 was a staff vehicle with a rear hull modified for map reading and carrying radios.
BA64SKh was a halftrack version sometimes fitted with skis in place of the front wheels for use in deep snow.
BA64zhD a rail version with the road wheels replaced with flanged steel.

Crew 2
Armament
One 7.62mm machine gun
Power plant 50hp four-cylinder GAZ-MM engine
Speed 50mph
Range 280 miles
Length 12ft
Width 5ft
Height 6ft 3ins

ZIS-5

The other widely used Russian truck was the ZIS-5, made at the Moscow factory, which began life under the name AMO. Between 1924 and 1932 they made about 6,000 of the AMO-15, a Fiat≠ based 11/2-ton truck which was used by the army as well as in civilian life. This was joined in 1931 by the AMO-3, a larger truck based on an American International Harvester pattern, with a 60bhp 4880cc six-cylinder engine of Hercules design.

In 1932 the AMO plant was renamed ZIS (Zavod lmieni Stalin) and the AMO-3 became the ZIS-3. Two years later it became the ZIS-5, of similar design but with a 73bhp 5550cc engine. A characteristic of both models was the windscreen divided about two thirds of the way across instead of in the centre, so that the driver had a wider field of vision than his passenger. These sturdy trucks remained in produc≠tion until 1955 in the Urals factory, built in 1941/42 when the German advance threatened Moscow. A large number of ZIS-5s were supplied to the Republican Army in the Spanish Civil War (1936-39) and were sold to civilian users after≠wards. The ZIS-5 chassis was used for carrying search≠lights, pontoon bridging equipment, tankers, snowploughs, air compressors and other special purpose vehicles. Later models, and probably all those made in the Urals factory, had flat topped mudguards like the GAZ-MMs.

There were several variants on the basic ZIS-5 design, including the ZIS-32 4x4 truck of 1941 and the ZIS-6 6x4 of 1935-45 and the ZIS-42 half-track.

Truck, 3-ton, 4X2, ZIS-5
Engine: ZIS-5 6-cylinder, 5550 cc, 73 bhp
Transmission: 4F1 R.
Brakes: mechanical.
Tyres: 34x7 (2DT)
Wheelbase: 3.81m
Length 6.06m
Width2.235m
Height 2.16m
Weight: 3100 kg.
Engine: ZIS-5 6-cylinder, 5550 cc, 73 bhp
Transmission: 4F1 R.
Brakes: mechanical.
Tyres: 34x7 (2DT)
Wheelbase: 3.81m
Length 6.06m
Width2.235m
Height 2.16m
Weight: 3100 kg.

GAZ67B

Produced at the GAZ factory at Gorky, the GAZ 67 was designed as a cross-country vehicle for transporting both personnel and light equipment. First produced in 1943, its design was greatly influenced by the US Bantam Jeep, many of which had been supplied to the Soviet Union under the Lend-Lease programme. It was powered by a Russian licence built copy of the Ford Model A engine which, while slightly heavier than the Jeep engine, produced about the same power. The performance of the GAZ67 was not quite as good as the Jeep's, particularly in terms of acceleration, which was poor. However, its simple and very basic design did not detract from the essential strength of the vehicle, which had very good cross-country mobility. The GAZ 67 was succeeded by the 67b in 1945. This had a slightly wider wheel track, 4ft 9in instead of 4ft 1in, and went to be produced in much greater numbers than the 67. The vehicle went on to see extensive service in Korea and Indochina, and formed the backbone of Soviet airborne divisions. Production ceased in 1953. Transmission consisted of four forward and one reverse gears.

Crew. 1
Weight. 1,220kg (2,684 lb)
Length 3.34m (10ft 11.33in)
Width 1.68m (5ft 6in)
Height 1.70m(5ft7in)
Range 750km (468 miles)
Powerplant. one GAl-A four-cylinder 3.28-litre petrol engine developing 54hp (40.3kW)
Maximum road speed 75km/h (46.8mph)
Fording 0.45m (1ft 6in)

M3 STUART

In the 30s a series of experimental combat cars and light tanks was produced for the US Army, culminating in the M2A4 which entered production in April 1940, a total of 365 eventually being built. Analysis of the war in France revealed the need for some improvements. Armour protection was increased and the hull was lengthened to cover the exhausts. In order to support the increased weight and lengthened hull it was decided to adopt the distinctive trailing idler wheel that was to become so characteristic of the Stuart series. The new vehicle was powered by a Wright Continental W-970-9A radial seven cylinder air-cooled, petrol-fuelled aero engine and was designated M3.

The original M3 was, like it's predecessors of all rivetted construction although a welded turret was soon introduced to save weight and this in turn was replaced by a part cast turret. At this stage a gyroscopic gun stabilizer was also introduced for the first time. Some late production M3s were fitted with Guiberson diesel engines and had hulls of welded construction.

Crew 4
Power plant either a Wright Continental radial air-cooled 250hp or a Guiberson radial air-cooled 220hp diesel engine
Maximum road speed 36mph
Armament
One 37mm main gun
Three .30cal machine guns, one mounted in the hull front, one co-axial with the main gun and one pintle mounted on the turret roof.
Armour 43mm max
Length 14ft 10.75ins
Width 7ft 4ins
Height 7ft 6.5ins

T8E1 Stuart based recce vehicle

By 1944 the Stuart was outclassed as a fighting tank, particularly in The European theatre, and was increasingly relegated to reconnaissance duties. In order to make the vehicle better suited to it's new role many M5 series vehicles had their turrets removed and replaced with a .50 cal Browning machine gun on a ring mount. This served to reduce the weight of the vehicle, thereby increasing it's performance, and also reduced the height of it's silhouette which made it harder to target. In the States this conversion recieved the limited standard designation T8E1. in the UK the M5 and M5A1, or Stuart VI, as they were both known were also converted in this way. The British also used turretless Stuarts as Kangaroo armoured personnel carriers, by fitting bench seats in the hull, and as gun tractors and armoured ambulances.

Crew 4
Armour 54mm front, 25.4mm side
Power plant two Cadillac V-8 petrol engines each producing 121hp
Maximum road speed 36mph
Armament
Three .30 cal Browning machine guns

M5 LIGHT TANK

The M5 arose from a claim by the Cadillac division of General Motors that twin V-8 Cadillac car engines could be used in place of the M3's standard Wright Continental. A shortage of the standard power plants had arisen from the increased demand for these engines for aircraft production and there were not sufficient Guiberson Diesel engines to make up the shortfall. To test Cadillac's claim an M3E2 prototype was fitted with the twin V-8, together with Cadillac's Hydra-Matic automatic transmission and after successfully completing a 500 mile proving run the the vehicle was ordered into production as the M5. Although the new vehicle retained the turret, chassis and suspension of the M3 the opportunity was taken to completely redesign the hull. The new hull was of improved ballistic shape, offered more space internally and it's simpler shape eased production. Maximum armour thickness was increased to 67mm and although this resulted in an increase in weight of 4.3 tons over the M3 to 16.5tons, the additional power of the new engine and the efficiency of the Cadillac transmission kept the maximum road speed at 36mph.

Crew 4
Weight 15.6tons
Armour 67mm max
Power plant two Cadillac V-8 petrol engines each producing 121hp
Maximum road speed 36mph
Armament
One 37mm main gun
Three .30 cal Browning machine guns, one mounted in the hull front, one co-axial with the main gun and one pintle mounted on the turret roof.

M3 Lee/Grant

The M3 was developed by the Americans following the realisation, based on observation of the armoured battles in France in 1940, that a more powerful armament would be required than that mounted on the M2 in development at the time. The M3 was shipped to British forces with different turret and other minor modifications and was known as the Grant. The Grant proved highly effective against the Afrika Korps in North Africa in its first actions in May 1942, and was popular with the tank crews of hard-pressed British forces. The original version known as the Lee was mainly used by US forces, but some were also supplied to Britain and to the USSR. Reliable and hard wearing, its only drawback was the limited traverse of the hull-mounted main gun. The M3 was produced in several models differing chiefly in the choice of power plant, and also served as the basis of numerous derivative vehicles.

Crew 6
Weight 27,240kg (59,928lb)
Dimensions
length 5.65m (18ft 6in)
width 2.72m (8ft 11in)
height 3.12m (10ft 3in)
Range: 193km (120 miles)
Armour: 12-38mm (0.47-1.5in)
Armament
One M2 L/28 or M3 l/38, 75mm hull-mounted gun
One 37mm turret-mounted gun
Three 7.62mm machine guns
Powerplant
Continental R-975-EC2 radial petrol engine developing 340hp (253.5kW)
Performance
maximum road speed 42km/h (26mph)
fording 1,02m (3ft 4in) vertical obstacle 0.6lm (2ft)
trench 1,9lm (6ft 3in)

MEDIUM TANK M4 SHERMAN

The new tank was to mount a 75 mm gun in a fully traversing turret, the first prototype, the Medium Tank T6, was rolled out in September 1941.

The hull was cast which not only made production quicker but also gave increased shot deflection. The turret mounted the M2 75mm gun as the intended M3 was still not available, but as on the M3 tank the gun was gyro-stabilised. A throwback to the days of the Medium Tank M2 was the fitting of two fixed machine-guns in the hull front but this was not done on production models. Another feature designed out on production models was the side escape doors as this not only made production easier but also provided a stronger hull. The version with welded plates became the M4 while the version with the cast hull became the M4A1. The production plans for the M4 expanded rapidly to meet the target of 1,000 tanks a month (later to be doubled).

The main problem yet again was the Wright Continental engine. This was really an aircraft engine and as the M4 programme got into its stride, so did a massive aircraft construction pro≠gramme, so calls on the Continental reached the stage where alternative engines had to be fitted to the M4s coming off the lines. This raised the usual crop of variants.

By the time production ended in 1946 well over 40,000 M4 tanks had been produced (this total includes all the M4 variants and special purpose vehicles) and with such a huge total made it was inevitable that there would be a large number of hybrid variants, and experimental vehicles.

Main M4 variants

M4
Version with Continental engine and welded hull. British Sherman I.

M4A1
First version to go into production. As M4 but with cast hull. British Sherman II.

M4A2
Fitted with twin General Motors diesel engines. British Sherman III.

M4A3
The Ford engine fitted to this ≠version was specially developed for tank use in the M4A3.
This version used the Chrysler Multibank engine and its bulk neces≠sitated a slightly lengthened hull. British Sherman V.

M4A5
It was fitted with a Caterpillar radial diesel engine in a lengthened hull.
This larger gun required the use of a larger turret, which was taken direct from the experimental Medium Tank T23. The 76mm gun was put into production in February 1944 and later versions were fitted with muzzle brakes.
Tanks fitted with the howitzer were used in the close support role with Medium Tank battalions. Put into production during early 1944.
Track covers were used with the new wider track.
One special tank version that rates a special mention is the Assault Tank M4A3E2. The extra weight reduced speed and the usual armament was the 75mm gun although some were retrofitted with the 76 mm weapon. Armour thickness was as much as 150 mm /5.9 inches on the turret front and up to 100 mm/ 3.9 inches on the hull.

M4A3
Crew 5
Weight in action 32,284 kg/71,175lb
Maximum road speed 47kph/29 mph
Maximum cross-country speed 32 kph/20 mph
Length with gun 7.51m/296 inches
Length less gun 6.27m/247 inches
Width 2.68m/105.5inches
Engine horsepower 450
Track width (vertical volute) 419 mm/ 16.5 inches
Track width (HVSS) 584 mm/23 inches
Wheel base 2.1m /83 inches
Armament
One 76 mm with 17 rounds
Two .30-inch machine-guns with 6,250 rounds
One .5-inch machine-gun with 600 rounds
Front armour 63.5 mm/2.5 inches
Side and front armour 38 mm/1.5 inches
Turret front armour 63.5 mm/2.5 inches

M22 Locust

Designed as an air transportable tank for use in airborne operations, the first T9 prototype was produced by Marmon-Herrington in 1941. This small tank mounted a 37 mm gun and as it had to be light, armour was thin. Further changes, mostly to save weight, resulted in the T9E1, which was standardised as the Light Tank (Airborne) M22 in early 1943. This remained in production until February 1944 but the M22 was destined never to go into action with the American forces as they lacked a suitable transport for it. As a result large numbers of M22s were issued under Lease-Lend to the British airborne units who had a glider large enough to carry the M22, the Hamilcar, and small numbers were used by the British during the Rhine crossings of March 1945. In British service the M22 was known as the Locust. In action the M22 was of very limited value. Its 37mm gun was ineffectual against most armoured vehicles in service after 1943 and fired a very weak HE round, and the thin armour offered minimal protection.

Crew 3
Weight in action 7,445kg/ 16,400lb Maximum road speed 64kph/40 mph
Maximum cross-country speed 48 kph /30 mph Road range 217km/135miles
Length 3.937m/155inches Width 2.159 m/85 inches Height 1.854 m/73 inches Engine horse power 162
Track width 286 mm/ 11.25 inches Wheel base 1.791 m/70.5 inches Armament
One 37 mm with 50 rounds
One .30-inch machine-gun with 2,500 rounds
Front armour 25 mm/0.98 inch

M24 CHAFFEE

By 1942 it was becoming obvious that the 37 mm gun was no longer viable as a tank weapon and a replacement for the M5 light tank would be needed since it was incapable of mounting a heavier weapon. During late 1943 a new vehicle, the Light Tank T24, was produced by Cadillac who had been involved in the development of the M5. The new tank retained several features of the old M5 such as the twin Cadillac engines and automatic transmission and mated them to a new hull with torsion bar suspension. The new turret mounted a 75 mm gun adapted from a heavy aircraft gun.

The T24 was standardised in May 1944 as the Light Tank M24 and was later given the name Chaffee. Full-scale production ensued and the first Chaffees entered service in late 1944. Some were shipped to Europe where they arrived to take a small part in the fighting that led to the end of the war in Europe. After the war the M24 went on to become one of the more important American tanks and it played a major role during the campaign in Korea.

Crew 5

Weight in action 18,370kg/40,500Ib Maximum road speed 56kph/35 mph

Maximum cross-country speed 40 kph/25 mph

Road range 161 km/100miles Length less gun 4.99m/ 196.5inches Length with gun 5.48m/216 inches

Width 2.94m/116inches Height 2.47 m/97.5 inches Engine horse power 220

Track width 406mm/16inches

Wheel base 2.44m /96 inches Armament

One 75 mm M6 with 48 rounds

Two .30-inch machine-guns with 4,125 rounds One .5-inch machine-gun with 420 rounds

Front armour 25.4 mm/ 1 inch

Side and rear armour 19 mm/0. 75 inch

Turret front armour 38 mm/1.5 inches

M26 PERSHING

The M26 Pershing was the result of a lengthy development process that started almost as soon as the Medium Tank M4 entered production. There was a long string of experimental vehicles of successively greater weight and striking power. The first of this line was the Medium Tank T20, which was developed into the T22. Then came the T23 that had a number of features that were tried on prototype vehicles and then introduced on to the Medium Tank M4 production lines. With the T25 the HVSS and vertical volute suspension were abandoned in favour of a new torsion bar suspension, but almost as soon as the T25 was produced the T26, with thicker armour and a 90 mm gun, was pressed into favour by the appearance in battle of the German Tiger and Panther tanks. Although these vehicles had been known to exist for some time it was not until 1944 that an effort to produce a heavy tank to counter them was made, and even then there were many who considered that the answer was the tank destroyer rather than the tank. The tank/tank destroyer argument continued until late 1944 when the German Ardennes offensive at last tipped the scales in favour of the heavy tank.

Crew 5
Weight in action 41,730 kg/92,000lb
Maximum road speed 48kph/30 mph
Maximum cross-country speed 8.4 kph/5.2 mph
Road range 148 km/92 miles
Length with gun 8.78m/346 inches
Length of hull 6.45m/254 inches
Height 2.76m/l09inches
Width 3.5m/138inches
Engine horsepower 500
Track width 609.6 mm/24inches
Wheelbase 2, 794 mm/110 inches
Armament
One 90 mm with 70 rounds
One .5-inch machine-gun with 550 rounds
Two .30-inch machine-guns with 5000 rounds
Front armour 101.6mm/4inches
Side armour 76 mm /3 inches
Rear armour 50.8 mm /2 inches
Turret front armour 101.6 mm /4 inches

M3 75MM GUN MOTOR CARRIAGE (HALF TRACK)

The Gun Motor Carriage M3 was an expedient tank destroyer and fire support vehicle; it mounted the 75mm M1897 A4 gun on the M3 mount, on the rear bed of the M3 half-track. Elevation was -10° to +29° and traverse 19° left and 21° right. 59 rounds of HE and AP/ APC ammunition were carried. No machine gun armament was fitted. The M3A1 gun motor carriage was identical, but used the M 5 mount, which reduced minimum elevation to -6.5° but gave 21° traverse each side. The crew consisted of the commander, driver, gunner and two-gun crew. The gun was marginal for the tank destroyer role from 1942, and the M3 was replaced by full≠ tracked vehicles, being declared obsolete in September 1944. It remained useful in the general support role and the British used it for that purpose until the end of the war.

Weight 9.09 tonnes
Armour front 12mm, side 8mm
Length 6.22m
Width 2.16m
Height 2.51m
Engine 128 horsepower
Road Speed 75km/h

M10 Wolverine

This vehicle used the chassis and power pack of the M4A2 (M10) or M4A3 (M10A1) Sherman, on which was mounted a superstructure with sloped armour, thinner than that of the tank and an open-topped turret carrying a 3" M7 gun and a pintle-mounted .50cal MG. Although the gun was better than the US 75mm tank gun and adequate for its time, the vehicle was something of a compromise and lacked the speed and agility of the later M18.

The reduced armour thickness did not buy an appreciable improvement in mobility, the lack of power turret traverse slowed engagement speed, and the absence of a coaxial or bow machine gun left it very vulnerable to enemy infantry. Nevertheless, it was the most numerous tank destroyer and served until the end of the war alongside the M18s and M36s. The British re-armed a proportion of their lend-lease M10s with the superior 17pdr gun to produce the Achilles.

Crew. 5
Weight 29,937kg (65,861 lbs)
Range. 322km (200 miles)
Armour 12-37mm (0.47-1.46in)
Armament
One 76.2mm M7 gun
One 12.7mm Browning machine gun
Power plant two General Motors six-cylinder diesel engines each developing 375hp (276.6kW)
Maximum road speed 51km/h (32mph)
Length 6.83m (22ft 5in)
Width 3.05m (10ft 0in)
Height 2.57m (8ft 5in)
Fording 0.91m (3ft)
Vertical obstacle 0.46m (18in)
Trench 2.26m (7ft 5in)

M36 JACKSON

The last of the wartime US tank destroyers was the heavily armed M36, which owed its greater firepower to a decision made in October 1942, to discover if the 90mm AA gun could be adapted to the anti-tank role in order to deal with the heavier enemy armour which was then starting to appear on the battlefield. Early tests with the M10 showed that, whilst the gun could be fitted satisfactorily, its increased length and weight caused consider≠able problems. Test firings proved satisfactory, but it was clear that a new turret was needed. Ford built two pilot models in March 1943 based on the M10A1 chassis. They were completed that September and proved very suc≠cessful, being given the designation GMC T71, and an order was placed for 500 vehicles. As with the other tank destroyers, the only machine gun armament was a .50cal weapon on an anti-aircraft mount. The turret had power traverse and, initially, an open top. A light armour cover retrofit kit was developed for fielded vehicles and later production vehicles featured a folding armour top on the turret.

Weight 26.4 tonnes
Armour front 55mm, side 25mm
Length 5.97m
Width 3.05m
Height 2.72m
Engine 375 horsepower
Road Speed 50km/h

M8 75MM HOWITZER

This was the smallest of the tank mounted self-propelled guns and was essentially the M5 light tank with the turret replaced by a larger open-topped unit armed with a 75mm M2 or M3 howitzer to provide mobile fire support. A large flash deflector tube that extended beyond the muzzle surrounded the barrel of the howitzer. The weapon could elevate from -20° to +40° and 46 rounds were carried. The two-man turret crew comprised the gunner on the left and the loader on the right. The driver and assistant driver (with duplicate controls) sat at the front. The secondary armament was a.50cal MG on a ring mount at the right rear of the turret. Cadillac produced 1,778 M8s between September 1942 and January 1944. They were widely used in the Pacific and European theatres in the headquarters companies of the medium tank battalions. The limited on board ammunition stowage was often supplemented with towed ammunition trailer. From 1944 they began to be replaced by l05mm howitzer-armed Shermans.

Crew 4
Weight (tonnes) 16.4tonnes
Front Armour front 30mm, side 25mm
Armament
One 75mm howitzer with 46 rounds
One .50cal machine gun
Length 4.34m
Width 2.24m
Height 2.29m
Engine twin Cadillac V8 petrol, producing 220 horsepower
Road Speed 60km/h
Range 130miles

Gun Motor Carriage M12

The Gun Motor Carriage M12 used the chassis of the M3 medium tank with the engine relocated from the rear to the centre of the vehicle. This left a platform at the rear on which was mounted the old 155mm M1917, M1917Al or M1918M1 gun (depending on availability) with a traverse of 14° each side and an elevation of-5° to +30°. The driver and commander sat inside the hull at the front, two gun crew sat to the left of the gun, and two on seats on the hinged spade at the rear. Only 10 projectiles and charges could be carried on the M12, so a similar vehicle, but without the gun and recoil spade, was built as the M30 cargo carrier to carry an additional 40 rounds of ammunition and additional gun crew. The vehicles operated in pairs, one M12 and one M30 per gun section. A total of 100 M12s was produced and they were retained for training in the US until June 1944 when 75 were overhauled and shipped to the European Theatre of Operations.

Weight (tonnes) 26.4
Armour front 50mm, side 20mm
Length 6.73m
Width 2.67m
Height 2.69m
Engine 353 hp, Wright Continental R-975 air-cooled radial
Max speed 12mph

M40 BIG SHOT, M4 8INCH HOWITZER AND M7 PRIEST

The M40 entered development in December 1943. It was based on the M4 Sherman tank chassis and mounted the 155mm 'Long Tom' gun. A heavy spade was attached to the rear, which could be dug into the ground to help absorb recoil after firing. The first production vehicles appeared in January 1945, and arrived just as World War II in Europe was ending. It continued in service, with a total of 311 being built, and saw the majority of its service in the Korean War (1950-53), where it proved an excellent weapon, and in Indochina with the French Army. The M40 appeared at a time when nuclear warfare was making its debut, and thus it was used extensively for post-war trials designed to provide protection against fallout for the crew, forming the blueprint of modern self-propelled vehicles. There was one variant of the M4, the M4 GMC which was essentially the same vehicle but mounting an 8in howitzer.

Nicknamed the 'Priest' by British crews because of its pulpit-shaped machine-gun turret at the front, the M7 grew from US experience with howitzers mounted on half-tracked vehicles. A fully tracked carriage was required, and the M3 tank was modified to fill the role. The British received many under the Lend-Lease scheme and deployed them for the first time at the 2nd Battle of El Alamein in 1942. Some measure of their popularity is suggested by the British order for 5500 to be delivered within one year of their first use. The drawback was that the howitzer was not standard British issue, and thus required separate supplies of ammunition. Mobile and reliable, the M7 fought to the end of the war with US forces. It was replaced in the British army by the Sexton SPG, which mounted a 25pdr and so did not require non-standard ammunition supplies. However it remained in service in the role of armoured personnel carrier as the Priest Kangaroo.

M4 Big Shot
Crew. 8
Weight 36,400kg (80,080lb)
Length 9.04m (29ft 8in); width 3.1 5m (10ft 4in); height 2.84m (9ft 4in)
Range 161km (100 miles)
Armour 12.7mm (0.5in) max
Armament one 155 mm gun
Power plant one Continental nine-cylinder radial piston engine developing 395hp (294.6kW)
Maximum road speed 386km/h (24mph)
Fording 1.067m (3ft 6in)
Vertical obstacle 0.61 m (2ft)
Trench 2.26m (7ft 5in)

M7 Priest
Crew: 5
Weight: 22,500kg (49,500Ib)
Length 6.02m (19ft gin)
Width 2.88m (9ft 5.25in)
Height 2.54m (8ft 4in)
Range 201km (125 miles)
Armour 25.4mm (1in) max
Armament
One 105mm howitzer
One 12.7mm machine gun
Powerplant. one Continental nine-cylinder radial piston engine developing 375hp (279.6kW)
Maximum road speed 41.8km/h (26mph)
Fording 1.21gm (4ft)
Vertical obstacle 0.61m (2ft); trench 1.91m (6ft 3in)

M18 HELLCAT

The history of the M18 dates back to December 1941 when the US Ordnance Department recommended the development of a light, tracked, tank destroyer. The original specification called for a 37mm gun mounted on a chassis utilising Christie type suspension, and fitted with a Wright Continental R-975 radial engine. Armour protection was to be minimal in order to promote good mobility. Two pilot models were constructed, the first being completed in mid 1942. Testing of the prototype and intelligence garnered from British experiences in the Western Desert led to major changes in the specification. The Christie suspension was replaced by a torsion bar design and the 37mm main gun was replaced by a series of successively larger weapons including the 57mm M1, and the 75mm M3 (mounted in a new turret on the second pilot model). Eventually in February 1943 the Tank Destroyer Command suggested the adoption of the 76mm M1 that was under development for fitting to the M4 Sherman. Six more pilot models, designated T70 GMC, were constructed, all mounting the 76mm gun.

Crew 5
Power plant Continental R-975 400hp radial engine
Maximum speed of 55mph
Range 105 miles.
Weight 18.25 tons
Maximum armour thickness was 12mm
Armament
One 76mm M1 main gun
One pintle-mounted .50cal Browning machine gun at the rear of the turret
Length 17ft 10ins (21ft 10ins including gun)
Width 9ft 5in
Height 8ft 5ins.

105 CAL. 50
LINKED A.P.I. M8
REPACK'D LOT LC-L-12283

M3 HALFTRACK

The M3's history dates back to the late thirties, when the US Cavalry made a request for a scout vehicle and artillery tractor with good cross-country performance. It was decided to take, as the basis of the new vehicle, the M3 scout car already being produced for the US Army by the White Motor Co. The chassis and body of the scout car were modified to accept track units in place of the rear wheels. These track units were based on a design originated by Adolph Kegresse whilst in the employ of the Czar of Russia in order to improve the performance of the Czar's fleet of cars in the deep Russian snow. With the advent of the Russian revolution Kegresse left Russia and returned to his native France where Citroen took up his ideas on half-track design and developed them for military applications. A whole series of half-track vehicles were produced for the French Army from the mid-20s until the war and so it was not unnatural for the designers of the new American vehicle to adopt such a tried and tested system . These track units were cheap and easy to produce, robust and hard wearing and required very little maintenance, especially when compared to the much more complex systems employed on half-track vehicles of the German Army.

Crew 3 men plus 10 fully equipped infantrymen
Power plant White 160 AX 6-cylinder petrol engine, producing 147hp
Maximum speed was 45 mph
Weight 9 tons.
Armament was one .30 or.50cal machine gun
Armour 12.72mm max
Length 20ft 2.5ins
Width 6ft 5.5ins
Height 7ft 5ins (M3A1 height 8ft 4ins).

WHITE SCOUT CAR M3

The M3A1 was designed and built by the White Motor Company, using a commercial-type 4x4 truck chassis, mounting an armoured body set on a channel-section frame. It was the last in a series of scout cars produced by that company and was produced in far greater numbers than any of its predecessors, 20,918 being produced during the war.

The driver and the commander sat in the front, while the personnel compartment in the rear could hold six troops. A skate rail encircled the top of the body interior, on which were mounted a .50cal MG and a .30cal MG. Armoured shutters, controlled from the driver's position, protected the radiator, and a drop-down armoured cover with direct-vision slots could protect the windshield. No overhead protection was provided except for a canvas cover. Designed as a scout car, the M3A1 was quickly found to be too unwieldy, too poorly protected and too weakly armed for that role. However, it quickly became a jack-of-all-trades and served a useful life as ambulance, repair vehicle, command vehicle, and general utility vehicle. 3,340 White Scout Cars were also supplied to the USSR.

Weight 3.85 tons
Armour front 12mm, side 8mm
Length 6.22m
Width 2.16m
Engine Hercules JXD petrol engine, producing 128hp
Height 2.51m
Road Speed 75km/h

M8 GREYHOUND

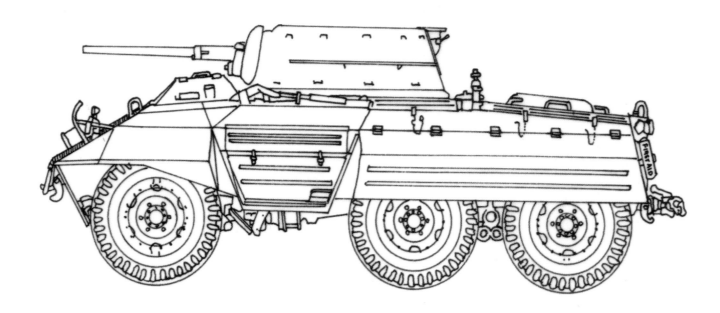

The best American armoured car of World War II was designed in response to a requirement by the Tank Destroyer Force for a 37mm Gun Motor Carriage. Intended to replace the 37mm Gun Motor Carriage M6, an anti-tank gun on an un-armoured 3/4ton truck,the T22, prototype of the M.8, was later re-classified as a light armoured car.

The T22 was designed by the Ford Motor Co. in competition with other 6x4 and 4x4 projects by Studebaker and Fargo. Out of these and many other armoured car designs at this time (some of which had even received large production orders) only the T17EI and the T22, which was completed in early 1942, modified as T22E2 and standardized as M8, remained to be produced in quantity after a critical survey had been carried out by the Special Armoured Vehicle Board.

Crew 4
Power plant Hercules JXD 6-cylinder petrol engine producing 110hp
Weight 7.5 tons
Maximum road speed 56mph
Armour 25mm max
Armament
One 37mm main gun
One co-axial.30 calibre machine gun
One skate ring or pintle-mounted .50calibre Browning machine gun (not always fitted).
Length 16ft 5ins
Width 8ft 4ins
Height 7ft 5ins

THE LVT FAMILY

The LVT was originally conceived as a rescue vehicle for use in the Okeechobee region of the Florida Everglades. The original prototype was built by engineer, Donald Roebling jr in 1935 at the suggestion of his financier father, John, who had witnessed the loss of life caused by the hurricanes that regularly swept the area. Many drowned in the swamp-lands as there was no way of reaching them in a boat or car. The Alligator as the new vehicle was known was designed to 'bridge the gap between where a boat ran aground and a car flooded out'. With war approaching this innovative new vehicle soon caught the attention of the US Navy, under who's aegis Roebling developed the amphibian for use as a ship to shore transport for use by the Marines.

The first military model the LVT1 was a large, open-topped un-armoured tracked amphibian designed mainly for the supply role. The LVT2 was an improved version that sought to remedy one of the LVT1s main shortcomings, its short mechanical life. The new power train was taken from the M3A1 light tank and a new suspension gave longer track life and a better ride on land. That still left one great shortcoming in the LVT configuration, that with the engine at the rear and the cargo hold in the centre, cranes had to be used to load and unload cargo, and embarked troops had to jump over the high sides to disembark. On some late production models the cab was armoured. The LVT4 was a major re-design. The engine was moved forward to a position just aft of the cab, creating space at the rear for a powered ramp. Not only troops, but jeeps and small artillery could be loaded and unloaded without difficulty. Unfortunately, it did not become available in numbers until 1945.

Extremely useful for logistical duties, the LVTs, even when fitted with extemporized armour, were extremely vulnerable when used in the assault role. To remedy this an armoured series was developed for use in beach assaults. The LVT was a highly successful vehicle that saw extensive use in the Pacific war and also in NW Europe. In all around 18,000 were produced of all models.

Landing Vehicle Tracked (Armoured) Mark IV 'Alligator'
The LVT(A)4 was developed from a long line of LVTs that started with the original Alligator, designed by Donald Roebling Jr, for use as a rescue vehicle in the swamps of the Florida Everglades. The vehicle was redesigned for military service at the request of the USMC in 1940 and the first, un-armoured, model was placed in production in November of that year. After the landings on

Tarawa in November 1943 it was realised that the LVT could be used to provide fire support during beach assaults and to provide the attacking troops with armour until conventional tanks could be brought ashore. To this end the LVT was provided with an armoured, fully enclosed hull on which was mounted the turret of the M3 Stuart light tank. In addition two machine gun positions were cut in the rear decking each with a 30cal. machine gun on ring mount and another machine gun was carried in the hull front.

The ability of these vehicles to cross reefs, traverse surf and then continue inland from the beach under fire made them invaluable in the island hopping campaigns of the Pacific theatre where they were used extensively by the U.S. Army and Marines. However in March 1944 it was decided that a heavier weapon was needed and so a successor to the LVT(A)1 was designed. The new vehicle had a similar hull to the LVT(A)1 but mounted the complete turret and 75mm howitzer of the M8 gun motor carriage. The two rear deck mg positions were also deleted to offset the greater weight

of the new turret. The new vehicle received the designation LVT(A)4. As well as serving in the Pacific LVT(A)4s were also to see action in Northern Italy and in the crossing of the Rhine.

Crew 6
Weight 18.3tons
Length 26ft 2in long
Width 10ft 8in wide
Height 10ft 2in
Armour Hull 13mm max, turret 44mm max
Power plant 250bhp Continental
Maximum speed of 16 mph on land and 7mph on water, the vehicle being propelled in water by its tracks, which are fitted with special 'W', shaped grousers.
Range 150 miles on land and 100 miles in water.
Armament
One 75mm M2 or M3 howitzer
One hull-mounted .50cal Browning machine gun and sometimes a second .50cal mg on a ring mount at the turret rear.

The vehicle shown bears the markings of a vehicle serving in the U.S. Army.Crew 6
Weight 18.3tons
Length 26ft 2in long
Width 10ft 8in wide
Height 10ft 2in
Armour Hull 13mm max, turret 44mm max
Power plant 250bhp Continental
Maximum speed of 16 mph on land and 7mph on water, the vehicle being propelled in water by its tracks, which are fitted with special 'W', shaped grousers.
Range 150 miles on land and 100 miles in water.
Armament
One 75mm M2 or M3 howitzer
One hull-mounted .50cal Browning machine gun and sometimes a second .50cal mg on a ring mount at the turret rear.

MACK NO

The Mack NO series was the main wheeled gun tractor built for the US Army in WWII and was intended primarily as a tractor for the 155mm gun and 8inch howitzer. Production began in 1940 with the Mack NO1, after acceptance trials of the pilot model NQ which differed from the production model in having a hard-top cab and a different type of front winch. The series progressed through successively improved models NO1, -2, -3, -6, and -7(-4 and -5 were experimental wreckers) during the course of the war. These vehicles were also supplied to the British Army.

Trucks of 4 tons and above were classed as 'heavy-heavy' in the US and the Mack NO was fairly typical of the design of this class of vehicle. The only unusual aspect of the design being that in the front driven axle the usual universal joint was dispenced with in favour of a bevelled double gear reduction in the axle ends which allowed for both driving and steering. As a result the axle housing was higher than the wheel hubs, providing extra ground clearance.

Power plant Mack EY six cylinder engine producing 159 horsepower
Weight 14.5 tons
Length 24ft 9ins
Width 8ft 7ins
Height 10ft 4ins (7ft 10ins minus tilts)

Diamond T and Rogers tank transporter trailer; M26 Dragon Wagon Tank Transporter

The Diamond T 12 ton prime mover M20 was originally designed in 1940 to meet the requirements of the British Purchasing Mission to the USA who were placing orders with various firms to replace or supplement existing equipment. The Diamond T was ordered for use in conjunction with the Trailer, M9, 45 ton, British Mk1 for the recovery and transport of tanks. This combination, known in the US under the designation Truck-Trailer, 45 ton, Tank Transporter, M19, was introduced in 1940/41. It first saw active service with the British Army in North Africa and was later also adopted for use by the US Army. The Diamond T M20 was equipped with a 20ton winch and a ballast body behind the cab. Early production vehicles had pressed steel cabs, but from August 1943 they were fitted with an open type cab and had provision for an AA machine gun ring mount. There were two models, the 980 and the 981. The 980 had a 300ft winch cable and two winch cable roller sheaves at the rear; the 981 had a 500ft winch cable, three winch sheaves at the rear and a roller assembly in the front bumper allowing the winch cable to be paid out to the front of the vehicle.

Crew 2
Weight 25.8 tons
Power plant Hercules DFXE 6 cylinder diesel engine, producing 185 bhp
Range 300 miles.
Length 23ft 4ins
Width 8ft 5ins
Height 8ft 5ins

The Trailer M9, British Mk1
Manufacturer Rogers Bros later also produced by other manufacturers
Maximum load 45tons
Length 30ft
Width 9ft 6ins
Height 5ft 2ins

Dodge WC54 Ambulance

In 1942 the 1/2 ton 4 x 4 range of vehicles as first introduced in 1936 was superseded by a new 3/4 ton range . Prototypes were produced by both Ford and Dodge. The latter becoming the large-scale producer of this type. The new models were sturdier and wider, had a lower silhouette and were fitted with high floatation combat tyres.

In addition to the standard weapons carrier, the 3/4 ton Dodges were supplied with a variety of body types, including the ambulance with a steel panel type body built by Wayne. The T214-WC54 could carry 4 stretcher cases or eight seated. It was used by all arms of the US military and was also supplied under lend-lease to the British Army. This body style was also used as a van for various applications.

Power plant Dodge T214 6-cylinder engine, producing 92hp
Weight 5.8 tons
Length 16ft 2.5ins
Width 6ft 5.75ins
Height 7ft 6ins.

T16 WINDSOR CARRIER

The original role envisaged for the Universal Carrier was for a fast, lightly armed vehicle to carry infantry across ground denied by small-arms fire and specifically, the Bren light machine gun and its team, hence the name Bren Gun Carrier. There was only one version of this vehicle named the "Bren Gun Carrier" but whatever the task, the entire family of vehicles was known by its users as Bren Carriers. In fact, numerous copies of the original Bren Carrier were produced and these were commonly known as the Universal Carrier.

Although over 40,000 Universal carriers were built in the UK during WWII it was felt that there was a need for still more of these vehicles. Accordingly, production of the Universal carrier was undertaken in Canada (29,000) and a modified version was produced in Australia and New Zealand. Meanwhile it was decided that a slightly larger version of the Universal Carrier would be desirable for tasks that required a greater capacity. This vehicle was longer than the Universal Carrier, having an additional road wheel on each side and was fitted with a more powerful engine.

Crew 2-5 depending on the role of the vehicle
Power plant Ford V8 95/100hp water-cooled petrol engine
Length 12ft 4ins;
Width 6ft 9ins;
Height 5ft 3ins.
Armour 12mm max.
Armament usually consisted of one .303cal Bren Gun.
Maximum road speed 31mph
Range 159 miles.

WARD LA FRANCE WRECKER

The common layout for US military trucks had been established in the 1930s and the favoured design was a normal control (long bonnet) truck with, in most cases, 6-wheel drive. Load capacity was usually underquoted to allow a large overload in emergencies. Dual rear wheels were the norm.

A huge range of such trucks was produced in load capacities ranging from 2 1/2 tons to 12 tons. The heavier trucks often filled the role of tractors for artillery or in some cases tank transporters. One such heavy duty 6 wheeled truck was built by Ward LaFrance and, unusually, only a recovery variant appeared. The first type, the M1, used a civilian pattern sheet metal cab but a later version, the M1A1, used an open cab with folding canvas top. Production of the M1A1 was shared between Ward LaFrance and Kenworth. The US forces and the British Army used both variants, the early versions served mostly with the British Army in the Middle East and Italy. Most were provided under the Lend Lease Agreement.

Power plant Continental 22R 6-cylinder engine, producing 145hp
Length 26 ft 6 in
Width 8 ft 3 in
Height 10 ft 2 in
Weight 25.2tons.

CHEVROLET 1.5TON TRUCK

Although trucks in this class had been pioneered by Marmon-Harrington, and were also produced by Dodge, International and GMC, by far the biggest producer was Chevrolet. During the war Chevrolet produced a total of about 160,000 one and one-half ton all wheel drive military trucks. All Chevrolet 1 1/2 ton trucks were fitted with enclosed cabs except the M6 bomb truck that was fitted with a soft-top cab and folding windscreen, and the airborne cargo truck that was modified to enable it to be dismantled for transport in C-37 aircraft. Only a few of these were modified from standard trucks in 1944.

The Chevrolet 1.5ton chassis was produced in two main series, the G-4100, produced from 1940-41, and the G-7100 from 1942-45. It was fitted with a variety of bodies including; cargo with and without winch, cargo long wheelbase, panel, telephone maintenance, telephone pole auger, crash rescue, dump with and without winch, and airfield lighting. Truck was also supplied as a chassis/cab for special bodies.

Weight 8 tons
Payload 1.5tons
Power plant 6 cylinder petrol engine, producing 93 horsepower
Maximum speed 48 mph
Length 19ft 3ins
Width 7ft 2ins
Height 8ft 8.5ins (7ft 3ins without tilt)

DUKW

The Duck was the result of a program initiated in 1942 to develop a vehicle to ferry stores from ships lying offshore to dumps within a beachhead without the aid of port facilities. The DUKW amphibious truck utilised the chassis of the standard American COE type 2.5ton 6x6 truck, fitted with a boat shaped body. It was designed by naval architects Sparkman and Stephens of New York in conjunction with the Yellow Truck and Bus Co, main producers of the 2.5ton truck (Yellow Truck and Bus Co became the Truck and Coach Division of General Motors in 1943). The new hull incorporated buoyancy tanks, a screw propeller and a rudder. The propeller and wheels could be powered together for entering and leaving the water.

Weight 15,000lbs
Capacity 2.25 tons or up to 40 men
Length 31ft
Width 8ft 3ins
Height 8ft 8ins with canopy raised, 7ft 6ins lowered.
Max speed 5 knots at sea and 50 mph on land.
It was sometimes fitted with an AA ring mount for a machine gun above the cab.

Jeep

The concept of a light military reconnaissance car was first formulated in the late 1930s and this led to a formal requirement from the US Army. In the summer of 1940 Karl K. Probst of the Bantam Car Co designed a vehicle to meet the US Army requirements and a prototype was constructed. A further 70 examples of an improved model followed and were purchased by the US Ordnance Department for testing. The trial vehicles performed well and the Ordnance Department decided to purchase a further 1,500 vehicles. Their request to do so, however was blocked by the Quartermaster-General on the grounds that Bantam's production facilities were too limited to fulfil the order. Two other manufacturers, Ford and Willys -Overland, had also been developing prototypes to meet the Army requirement. In spite of the fact that neither had been completed by the time the Bantam was tested, all three companies received contracts, on completion of their respective prototypes, to produce 1,500 vehicles, much to the annoyance of Bantam. These vehicles were known as the Bantam 40BRC, Willys MA and Ford GP and were subject to further tests.

Weight 2,450lb
Power plant 4-cylinder Go Devil petrol engine, producing 54 hp
Maximum speed was 50mph.
Length 11ft
Width 5ft 2ins
Height 6ft with the hood erected, 4ft 6ins with the hood down and windscreen folded.

HARLEY-DAVIDSON WLA

The WLA was a standard production machine, adapted for military service. The modifications included: the fitting of a rear carry rack, leather panniers, front and rear crash bars, a windscreen, a scabbard for a Thomson machine gun or rifle on the right front fork leg, and a crank case guard, and the application of an all over service livery with a black exhaust system. The big Harley stood up admirably to the rigours of military use; it was standard practice to drop the bike on it's side in certain situations, and bikes serving in armoured divisions were sometimes transported, lashed to the engine decks of the tanks. That neither of these practises seemed to have any detrimental effect is a testament to their rugged construction and reliability. The WLA was successful and well liked in service, being used for solo dispatch, escort, convoy control and military police duties. Their effectiveness was reflected in their production figures, over 89,000 being produced in the period 1939-44. Of these around 60,000 went to the US forces and the majority of the remainder went to the British and Commonwealth Armies, where they continued in use until the late 50s.

Weight 575lb loaded
Power plant Harley-Davidson 740cc sv V-twin engine, producing 23hp
Maximum speed 60 mph.
Length 7ft 4ins
Width 3ft .25in
Height 3ft 5ins

M4 HIGH SPEED ARTILLERY TRACTOR

Development of what was to become the M5 began in 1941 when the T20 and T21 were developed using the tracks and suspension of the M3 tank. In October 1942, the T21 was standardised as the M5, designed to tow 105mm and 155mm howitzers as well as their crew and equipment. Five different models were produced in all, differing mainly in their track and suspension. The vehicle entered production in 1942 and was built by International Harvester. A winch was fitted as standard and roller under the winch allowed it to be used to pull vehicles to front or to the rear. The vehicle did not outlast World War II very long in the US Army, but it continued to serve with the ies of Austria, Japan, Yugoslavia and Pakistan for many years 1945.

Crew 1 + 10
Weight. 13, 791kg (30,340 lb)
Length 5.03m (16ft 6in)
Width 2.54m (8ft 4in)
Height 2.69m (8ft 10in)
Range 241km (150miles)
Armament one 12.7mm Browning machine gun in anti-aircraft mount
Power plant one Continental R6S72 six-cylinder petrol engine developing207hp (154kW)
Maximum road speed 48km/h (30mph)
Fording 1.3m (4ft 4in);
Vertical obstacle 0.7m (2ft 3in)
Trench 1.7m (5ft 6in)

STUDEBAKER M29 WEASEL

Designed by Studebaker and introduced in 1943, the diminutive 2.68ton Weasel tracked carrier was originally designed for use over snow as a result of experience in Alaska and the Aleutians. The early M28 version had 15in tracks, the later M29 had wider 20in ones and the engine was relocated to the rear of the vehicle. It had a cargo capacity of only 1,200lbs but could tow 4,200lbs. The third version of the Weasel was the M29C this was fully amphibious and was a modification of the basic cargo carrier M29, featuring bow and stern extensions, air tanks, track side panels and cable-actuated rudders. It was also used by the British (' Amphibian, 10-cwt, Tracked, GS'). Total production was approx. 15,000 units.

Crew 2-4
Power plant Studebaker 6-cylinder Champion petrol engine, producing 65bhp,
Transmission 3F1RX2
Range 175miles
Cargo capacity 1,200lbs
Length 126ins
Width 66ins
Height 71ins with tilt raised, 54ins tilt lowered
Laden weight 454lbs.

DODGE WC52 WEAPONS CARRIER (LATE MODEL)

Introduced in 1942, the Dodge T214 0.75-tonnes (0.75-tons) truck was the successor to the T215 and was slightly wider and lower with larger wheels and stronger suspensions. Referred to as 'Beeps' (a contraction of 'Big Jeeps), the T214 had a range of body types for different roles: weapons carrier, winch-equipped, ambulance, radio vehicle, command reconnaissance vehicle and repair vehicle. There were a number of different styles of body work including station wagon, open cab flatbed, panel van, knock down ambulance, mobile repair truck, and command car. The common by far was the weapons carrier WC51 and WC52, being fitted with a front mounted winch. The fact that vehicles are still in use around the world today is a tribute sturdy design of these vehicles, which were characterised by maintenance and an ability to take a lot of punishment. mission consisted of four forward and one reverse gears.

Crew 1
Weight 2,449kg (5,388 lb)
Length 4.24m (13ft 11in)
Width 1.99m (6ft 6.5in)
Height 2.07m (6ft 9.5in)
Range 450km (281 miles)
Power plant Dodge T214 six-cylinder petrol engine developing 92hp (68,6kW)
Maximum road speed 110km/h (68.75mph)
Fording 0.5m (1ft 7in)

STAGHOUND

The Staghound was developed in response to a US Army requirement for a light armoured car in the early years of World War II. However, by the time the vehicle was ready for production, the American army had selected the M8 Greyhound as its standard armoured car and all production models of the T17 were shipped to British and Commonwealth forces. The vehicle was fast, manoeuvrable and easy to operate and maintain. It first saw combat in Italy in 1943, and immediately proved a success. The Mk II mounted the complete turret and armament of the M8 Gun Motor Carriage 75mm howitzer and the Mk III was fitted with the turrets and 75mm guns from Crusader tanks. These were readily available since the Crusaders, being obsolete as gun tanks were being modified as gun tractors and AA tanks. A popular vehicle, the Staghound continued in service with the British for several years after the end of World War II.

Crew 5
Weight 13,920kg (30,624Ib)
Dimensions
Length 5.486m (18ft 0in)
Width 2.69m (8ft l0in)
Height 2.36m (7ft 9ins ≠
Range 724km (450 miles)
Armour 8mm (0.31in) maximum
Armament
One 37mm gun
Three 7.62mm machine guns
Powerplant two GMC six-cylinder petrol engines each devel
97hp (72kW)
Maximum speed 89km/h (55mph)
Fording 0.8m (2ft 8in)
Vertical obstacle 0.533m (1ft 9in)